Bankruptcy Prediction through Soft Computing based Deep Learning Technique

Arindam Chaudhuri • Soumya K. Ghosh

Bankruptcy Prediction through Soft Computing based Deep Learning Technique

Springer

Arindam Chaudhuri
Samsung R & D Institute Delhi
Noida, Uttar Pradesh, India

Soumya K. Ghosh
Department of Computer Science
and Engineering
Indian Institute of Technology Kharagpur
Kharagpur, West Bengal, India

ISBN 978-981-10-6682-5   ISBN 978-981-10-6683-2   (eBook)
https://doi.org/10.1007/978-981-10-6683-2

Library of Congress Control Number: 2017959591

Printed on acid-free paper

This Springer imprint is published by Springer Nature
The registered company is Springer Nature Singapore Pte Ltd.
The registered company address is: 152 Beach Road, #21-01/04 Gateway East, Singapore 189721, Singapore

To our families and teachers

Preface

Bankruptcy prediction has been actively studied in industrial and financial institutions in the recent past. The problem has been investigated through statistical and machine intelligence prediction techniques. Here, complex hierarchical deep architectures (HDA) are proposed for predicting bankruptcy. HDA are formed through fuzzy rough tensor deep stacking networks (FRTDSN) with structured hierarchical rough Bayesian (HRB) models. FRTDSN is formalized through TDSN and fuzzy rough sets. HRB is formed by incorporating probabilistic rough sets in structured hierarchical Bayesian model. Then FRTDSN is integrated with HRB to form the compound FRTDSN-HRB model. HRB enhances the prediction accuracy of the FRTDSN-HRB model. The experimental datasets are adopted from the Korean construction companies, American and European nonfinancial companies and UCI Machine Learning Repository bankruptcy database. The research revolves around the impact of choice toward cut-off points, sampling procedures, and business cycle accuracy for bankruptcy prediction techniques. Misclassification can often lead to incorrect predictions resulting in prohibitive costs to both investors and the economy. The selection of cut-off points and sampling procedures affects the model rankings. The results lead to the fact that empirical cut-off points derived from training samples result in minimum misclassification costs for all the techniques. FRTDSN-HRB achieves superior performance as compared to other statistical and soft computing models. The experimental results are given in terms of several standard statistical parameters revolving different business cycles and mid-cycles for the datasets considered.

Contents

List of Figures

List of Tables

About the Authors

Arindam Chaudhuri is currently a Data Scientist at the Samsung R&D Institute, Delhi, India. He has worked in industry, research and teaching in the field of machine learning for the past 16 years. His current research interests include pattern recognition, machine learning, soft computing, optimization and big data. He received his MTech (2005) and PhD (2011) in Computer Science from Jadavpur University, Kolkata, India, and Netaji Subhas University, Kolkata, India, respectively. He has published 2 research monographs and over 40 articles in international journals and conference proceedings. He has served as a reviewer for several international journals and conferences.

Soumya K. Ghosh is a Professor in the Department of Computer Science Engineering at the Indian Institute of Technology, Kharagpur, India. His current research interests include pattern recognition, machine learning, soft computing, cloud applications and sensor networks. He received his MTech (1996) and PhD (2002) in Computer Science Engineering from the Indian Institute of Technology Kharagpur, India. He has over 25 years of experience in industry, research and teaching. He has published 2 research monographs and over 100 articles in international journals and conference proceedings. He has served as a reviewer for several international journals and conferences.

Chapter 1
Introduction

Bankruptcy prediction [1, 2, 3] can be defined as the process where bankruptcy is projected along with several financial distress measures in corporate institutions and public firms. It is an active research area in business and mathematical finance. The importance of bankruptcy is mainly attributed to the creditors and investors in assessing the likelihood that an organization can become bankrupt. Bankruptcy investigation is generally expressed as function of the data availability. For public organizations that were either bankrupt or not, there are a large number of accounting ratios [4] that indicate danger which are calculated and other relevant explanatory variables [3] which currently exist. As a result of this, the topic of bankruptcy is well versed toward testing the complex and data-intensive prediction techniques [5].

Corporate bankruptcy prediction [1, 4] is an ever-growing process of interest to investors or creditors, as well as borrowing institutions. Timely recognizing the firms' moving toward failure is often desired. Bankruptcy can be considered as the state where the firm is not able to satisfy the debts and requests of the court of law to restructure its debts or liquidate its assets. The debtor's property is overtaken by the receiving person so that the creditors' are benefitted. A timely prediction is considered as gold for any business which helps to evaluate risks in order to prevent bankruptcy [1, 6]. The substantial research work has been performed toward predicting bankruptcy [1–4, 6–26]. There are several alarming signs of affecting financial disaster that forces any manager to behave in a preemptive way toward preventing things from getting worse. The financial disaster signs become obvious the way before the bankruptcy comes into picture [1]. Financial disaster starts when any company does not satisfy its scheduled payments. The major bankruptcy causes [5] are generally categorized as economic, financial, neglect, fraud, disaster, and others. Weakness in the industry leads to economic factors. The excess in debt leads to financial factors. The misjudgment takes the shape of financial difficulties. Managerial neglect arises when errors and misjudgments grow. During the late 1990s, the fraud in corporates became a major concern. There are no robust models

© Springer Nature Singapore Pte Ltd. 2017
A. Chaudhuri, S.K. Ghosh, *Bankruptcy Prediction through Soft Computing based Deep Learning Technique*, https://doi.org/10.1007/978-981-10-6683-2_1

available in the literature that identifies corporate fraud. The reason behind corporate failure is the financial disaster which includes human faults.

Bankruptcy is restricted exclusively toward any particular economic condition. Globalization spreads economic disaster fire involving economies after it witnesses its severe impact. Several countries have developed their own bankruptcy prediction models in order to tackle financial disaster consequences. Predicting corporate failure through previous economic data is a hot financial business topic [1, 4, 5, 6, 12]. The solution is often given through the discriminant function. In the United States, bankruptcies have grown over the past two decades. The 20 out of 25 bankruptcy filings in the United States happened during this phase. A good amount of work has been concentrated toward the corporate failure prediction. The techniques developed are based on decision science and artificial intelligence models. During this disaster phase, the three important decision science models, viz., Bayesian [19], hazard [20], and mixed logit [27], have been used toward predicting the bankruptcy. These techniques have mathematical benefits over the other prediction techniques.

Deep learning networks [28] are an emerging research area in soft computing domain. They have been used for several machine intelligence tasks [29] in the last few years. Deep learning networks are third-generation artificial neural networks (ANNs) which achieve superior performance than the traditional ANNs. They are related to machine learning-based algorithms that model high-level data abstractions through multiple layers of processing with complex structures and nonlinear transformations. The deep architectures behave superbly in terms of variables toward scaling the complex calculations. This makes them appreciably strong in achieving considerable generalization with comparatively less data volumes. Some of the common activities possessed by artificial intelligence (AI) systems include learning, reasoning, and self-correction. ANNs with several hidden layers learn complex operations but generally suffer from good learning algorithm. Support vector machines (SVMs) [30] facilitate the learning process through statistical learning theory and overcome several drawbacks of ANN. But due to shallow architectures, SVMs encounter several obstructions. The deep architectures address several inherent problems available with other architectures [29] where there is only one hidden layer. The hidden layers follow linear layers leading to the output [5] in supervised learning. Several thin architectures such as gaussian mixtures, radial basis functions (RBF), and ANN with one nonlinear hidden layer are universal approximators that model any operation. But the accuracy concerns remain a major issue in such representations. The deep learning algorithms consider a broad set of aspects [29] in order to achieve deeper insight into biological representations that are useful in several real-life applications. They learn multiple representation levels. Their abstraction helps them to sketch useful inferences from different data types.

In this research work, we propose complex hierarchical deep architectures (HDA) for bankruptcy prediction from various datasets. HDA are formed through fuzzy rough tensor deep stacking networks (FRTDSN) with structured hierarchical rough Bayesian (HRB) models. The deep learning model considered here is tensor deep stacking networks (TDSN) [31]. TDSN is consists of several stacked blocks.

Each block has maps bilinearly from hidden to the output layer by means of the weight tensor higher-order statistics. For parameter estimation the learning algorithm uses weight matrices and tensors which is performed by convex subproblem. The computational power of TDSN is increased through fuzzy rough sets such that FRTDSN is evolved. The prediction power of FRTDSN is further enhanced by HRB. HRB are formed by incorporating probabilistic rough sets [2] in structured hierarchical Bayesian model. HRB makes use of hyperparameter and hyperprior in order to achieve the posterior distribution. The hyperparameter and hyperprior are the parameters and distribution of a priori distribution, respectively. Finally FRTDSN is integrated with HRB to form the compound FRTDSN-HRB model. The experimental datasets are adopted from the Korean construction companies [32], American and European nonfinancial companies [33], and UCI Machine Learning Repository bankruptcy database [34]. The FRTDSN-HRB performance is also compared with fuzzy support vector machines (FSVMs) [3, 35] and other statistical models [2]. The experimental results are highlighted in terms of important statistical parameters encompassing different business cycles and mid-cycles for the considered datasets.

The monograph work is structured in the following manner. The research goals are presented in Chap. 2. This is followed by related works on bankruptcy prediction in Chap. 3. Chapters 4 and 5 highlight the bankruptcy prediction methodology and need for risk classification, respectively. In Chap. 6 the experimental framework revolving FRTDSN-HRB model for bankruptcy prediction is discussed. The next chapter presents the experimental datasets used in this research. In Chap. 8 the experimental results are illustrated. Finally in Chap. 9, conclusions are placed.

Chapter 2
Need of This Research

All companies are subjected to bankruptcy during the course of their lifetime. In recession companies may go in a bankrupt state. The important advantage lies in recognizing associated problems and appreciating the process that goes to bankruptcy and benefits from them. The research monograph addresses this issue. It is achieved by investigating bankruptcy datasets of Korean construction companies [32], American and European nonfinancial companies [33], and UCI Machine Learning Repository bankruptcy database [34]. This research aggregates both practical and empirical interest. From empirical perspective it uses significant concepts. Considering the practical viewpoint, this provides the utilization elements. All stakeholders involved with the company are affected by bankruptcy. Predicting bankruptcy involves many challenges. The first challenge starts with the technique selection which is achieved through literature review and brainstorming the techniques. The literature review is presented in Chap. 3. The methodology is highlighted in Chap. 6. The appropriate data is collected to validate the chosen technique. The data preprocessing is performed with respect to the chosen technique. This step is very important for the research because the input data quality affects the results. After the data are collected and preprocessed, they are applied to the proposed technique to get the results. The results are then interpreted and compared with other models. This is followed by refinement of the model in accordance with the desired benchmark levels. Then several tests are conducted to verify the overall fitness of the model.

2.1 Motivation

The major prima face in selecting bankruptcy prediction for research is that it permits working on practical and empirical aspects of the life of any firm. The study of bankruptcy has become the most sorted after research topic as a result of the global economic crisis. Many aspects of business world are considered which if

© Springer Nature Singapore Pte Ltd. 2017
A. Chaudhuri, S.K. Ghosh, *Bankruptcy Prediction through Soft Computing based Deep Learning Technique*, https://doi.org/10.1007/978-981-10-6683-2_2

achieved will be always good to the entire business community. It captures and understands elements and reasons resulting in corporate default. Another motivation is to devise an abstract mathematical technique toward bankruptcy prediction of different companies present in global economy. The model once developed and implemented will help analysts to understand different factors leading to bankruptcies. This entire work is based on the following research questions:

(a) How the bankruptcy of any company is predicted and how to avoid payment defaults?
(b) What are the different variables leading to bankruptcy in a specific industry?

2.2 Contributions

The different contributions made by this research works are:

(a) An in-depth literature review of the research done on bankruptcy prediction.
(b) The investigation proposes compound hierarchical deep architecture model, viz., FRTDSN-HRB which integrates deep learning models with structured HRB models in order to predict bankruptcy in Korean construction companies, American and European nonfinancial companies, and UCI Machine Learning Repository bankruptcy database.
(c) The model's superiority is highlighted through comparing it with other techniques.

Chapter 3
Literature Review

The factors which contribute to corporate bankruptcy know-how generally come from economics and business management. The bankruptcy prediction problem was first studied by Smith and Winakor in 1935 [36] and by Merwin in 1942 [37]. Another notable study was performed by Altman in 1993 [1]. These studies pointed that the failing organizations have significantly different ratios than the successful ones. This fundamental aspect provided a significant breakthrough and offered positive directions for further research. In 1965 Hickman [38] studied about ratios of large asset-size organizations that went through difficulties in meeting their obligations. In 1966 Beaver [39] studied the bankruptcy prediction problem through ratio analysis. Beaver's work is considered as one of the classical works in bankruptcy prediction. He argued on the use of multivariate analysis and commented on the use of univariate analysis in order to predict corporate bankruptcy. Neter [5] however strongly supported the use of multivariate analysis for this problem. Beaver discovered that till 5-year period before the organization's failure, the number of ratios differed from corresponding non-failed organization. He viewed the organization as reservoir of liquid assets, where inflows represent the supply and outflows represent the drain. The organization's solvency is defined in probability terms where the company is not able to pay its obligations and the reservoir becomes empty. Beaver stated four propositions through this framework, viz., (1) the smaller the probability of failure, the reservoir becomes large; (2) the smaller the probability of failure, the net liquid asset operations flow becomes large; (3) the greater the probability of failure, the amount of debt held is large; and (4) the greater the probability of failure, the operations fund expenditures become large. The ratios by Beaver are categorized into six groups consisting of 30 ratios. These ratios are experimented with 79 pairs of bankrupt and non-bankrupt organizations, through the univariate discriminant analysis. The working capital funds flow/total assets and net income/total assets were considered as the best discriminators. About 90% and 88% of the business cases were correctly identified by these cases. These ratios provide pointers toward bankruptcy probability which measure profitability, liquidity, and solvency. However, it was not clear which ratios provided the best

© Springer Nature Singapore Pte Ltd. 2017

A. Chaudhuri, S.K. Ghosh, *Bankruptcy Prediction through Soft Computing based Deep Learning Technique*, https://doi.org/10.1007/978-981-10-6683-2_3

explaining power. The above works mentioned different ratios as the most effective ones. The aspects which deserved the most attention are (1) the most important bankruptcy prediction ratios and (2) the weights to be attached with these ratios (3) objectively attaching these weights.

In 1968 Altman [4] proposed the Z-score model for bankruptcy prediction. This model is based on five variables. It uses multiple discriminant analysis (MDA) which has very strong predictive power. It is a statistical technique that classifies observations into categories with respect to the observations' attributes. There are various studies that validated the results of Altman's study through which MDA became a common approach in predicting bankruptcy. In later years the Z-score model was gradually updated. Some of the notable pointers in this direction are:

(a) The Z-score model generally focusses on relatively small companies. With the increase in the size of the bankrupt companies, there is requirement for a need model which is able to predict business failure with the bigger companies.
(b) There is a requirement for a model which behaves as customary as possible in accordance with the temporal data.
(c) Prior to this the concentration was on specific industries. The new model should cater the needs of different industries.
(d) The new model should be applied with respect to the future data.
(e) It allows to test and assess different aspects of the discriminant analysis.

The significant woks in this direction are by Platt et al. in 1990 and 1991 [5], Weiss in 1981 [40], and Zavgren et al. in 1983 [25]. In 1977 Altman et al. [6] proposed the ZETA model that is easily applicable to bigger companies. The ZETA model worked well with classifying the bankruptcy. In the succeeding years, several researchers used Beaver [39] and Altman [1] models in their works. In 1972 Deakin [41] proposed an alternative bankruptcy prediction model based on Beaver and Altman models. He captured the best of both Altman and Beaver models. The results by Beaver had greater prediction ability, and results by Altman showed more intuitive analysis. The linear combination of the 14 ratios used by Beaver was identified by Deakin. This best predicted company's failure in each of the 5 years failure prior. Some other notable works based on Altman and Beaver works are Wilcox [42] and Edmister, Libby, and Scott [5]. The bankruptcy prediction problem has also been approached through Bayesian [19], hazard [20], and mixed logit [27] models. The Bayesian model uses Bayesian statistics where previous knowledge is fine-tuned through estimates collected from mathematical facts. Then posterior probability is calculated. This model is transparent and simple to understand. The hazard model provides improvement over logit model such that in hazard model, bankruptcy is modeled not as process at a point of time but as process that ends with company's life. The mixed logit model supersedes over logit model such that both observed and unobserved information are taken care of. Begley et al. in 1996 [43] reached to similar results as Altman's 1968 [4] and Ohlson's 1980 [17] models. Robertson et al. in 1991 [5] argued that it could not be assumed that model's predictive power can move to industries. In 1999 Sung et al. [5] illustrated that the ZETA model is considered as the most accepted multidimensional model. The ZETA model has higher power of discrimination with reasonable parsimony. It considers accounting and stock market data as well as debt variables and earnings. Ohlson coined the logit analysis model for bankruptcy prediction in 1980. His study was based on the works of White and Turnball and Santomero and Vinso [5]. This was one of the first systematic developments of the probabilistic failure estimates. The probability of organization's failure was examined through important factors like the organization's size, the measures of the organization's financial structure, performance measures, and current liquidity measures. Ohlson used nine independent variables to predict the failure probability with certain success. Other important works in the logit and probit models include Martin et al. [15], Wiginton et al. [24], Zavgren et al. [25], and Zmijewski et al. [26] in the 1980s. The bankruptcy prediction models are also assessed considering the specific time period from the sample chosen. The accounting variables have dynamic distribution [44, 45] such that the models are sample specific [7]. Zmijewski's 1984 [26] and Ohlson's 1980 [17] models were reestimated by Grice et al. in 2001 using other periods of time. It was concluded that each model's accuracy declined from the period of 1988–1991 to 1992–1999. He discovered that Ohlson's model was closely related to classification by the industry which was not with Zmijewski's model. In assessing the bankruptcy prediction models, Zmijewski recognized two sampling errors. The sample bias is considered for the first model. Bankruptcy prediction analysis procedure for sampling recognizes bankrupt and non-bankrupt observation groups. The prediction power becomes upwardly biased as the selected probability for the bankruptcy samples moves away from population bankruptcy probability. The choice-based bias and results were in line with Zmijewski's facts as argued by Platt et al. in 2002 [5]. The sample selection bias is related to the second sampling error. Here incomplete data observations are eliminated by the sampling procedures. The correlation between bankruptcy and missing data observations is established through bivariate normal distribution by Zmijewski. There is a higher probability of bankruptcy for the missing data observations as observed by him. In 2005 Beaver et al. [9] raised the intangible assets' importance which increased over time. This happened because of the assets based on the technology. The financial derivative markets suffered the 1990s explosion. The financial derivatives are used as leverage alternative which underestimates companies' leverage ratios. Begley et al. in 1996 [43] also stressed the importance of leverage variables. Beaver et al. highlighted the increasing discretion degree associated with the gamut of the financial statements. These developments directly impacted financial ratios which underestimate the prediction power of the bankruptcy models with financial variables as inputs. The financial ratios for organizations are another important area which has been applied to bankruptcy prediction. Some of the significant works in this direction are by Ramser et al. [46], Fitzpatrick et al. [47], and Winakor and Smith [48] in the 1930s. The important statistical models which are applied to predicting bankruptcy is the ruin model of gambler by Wilcox et al. [42], option pricing theory by Merton et al. [49] in 1970s,

Koh and Tan [50], Atiya et al. [51], Baek and Cho [52], Becerra et al. [53], Durga and Dimitri [54], Pramodh and Ravi [55], Purvinis et al. [56], Ravi et al. [57], and Shah and Mirza [58].

During the past four decades, other AI-based techniques like recursive partitioning, ANN, genetic algorithms (GA), decision tree, etc. have gained considerable popularity toward the bankruptcy prediction problem. These methods offer better solutions over the classical statistical techniques. Recursive partitioning [5] is an inductive learning based on supervised learning technique. Here the training of the supervised learning model is based on certain dependent variables. Inductive learning builds decision trees which learn from examples by generalization process. The decision tree partitions the dataset input space into subsets. Each subset is partitioned into sub-subsets by the recursive partitioning procedure. By this process a tree is built with root at the top and mutually exclusive regions and leaves at the bottom. All the leaves are either labeled as bankrupt or non-bankrupt. This process requires only little prior knowledge. In 1986 Quinlan [59] proposed the ID3 algorithm which learns trees by constructing them in a top-down manner. Each time the algorithm decides the most important variable. This is achieved through certain statistical tests [5] in order to determine how well the training examples are classified. The decision trees are built by partitioning the training dataset into subsets recursively when the leaf nodes contain either bankrupt or non-bankrupt values. Through the tree any new organization is easily evaluated. Another significant work in recursive partitioning for bankruptcy prediction analysis is by Frydman et al. [60]. ANN [61] provides another classification chance for the bankruptcy prediction problem. They perform classification task in the way which is very much identical to human decision-making, viz., whether an organization is bankrupt or non-bankrupt. ANNs are good classifiers in many real-world classification problems. They have nonlinear and nonparametric adaptive learning properties. ANNs are described through a number of interconnected layers with simple logical units often dented as nodes. These networks are coined in the 1950s and are inspired by the way the human brain works. ANN are however dependent on the choice of proper training methods. With the reformulation of the backpropagation algorithm by Rumelhart et al. [62] in 1986, this dependency was removed. In feedforward ANN the logical units are called perceptrons which model the human brain's neuron. This neuron activates on the output side when a certain threshold is achieved. The input vector is controlled through bias factor at the previous layer. The output is transfer function which is nonlinear and differentiable in nature. The logistic function, hyperbolic tangent function, etc. are the commonly used activation functions. When ANN is used for the bankruptcy prediction problem, the information on explanatory factors is taken at input nodes via input layers. At the hidden layer, the weighted interconnections are done through the input nodes. The nodes at the hidden layer collect and process the information and determine the failure probability. In 1990 Odom and Sharda [63] first used ANN toward the bankruptcy prediction problem. The other significant works include Tam and Kiang [64]. GA motivated by the Darwin's theory of evolution [65] are stochastic derivative-free optimization techniques where search is performed through very large spaces. They have inductive nature. The possibility of the search getting trapped in a local minimum is very small since many points are used and they are stochastic in nature. They optimize on continuous and discrete functions. GA are based on probabilistic optimization rules. They work with strings which represent the parameters. GA work with a population which is evaluated at every generation. The working hypothesis is represented through chromosomes in each generation which are evaluated according to their fitness value. The chromosomes with the highest fitness value immediately get placed in the new population. The others create offspring individuals through genetic operators such as crossover and mutation. GA have been actively used for variable selection in ANN within the bankruptcy prediction problem framework. Some of the significant works of GA in bankruptcy prediction include Lensberg et al. [66] and Sengupta and Singh [67]. The fuzzy classifiers are applied to predicting bankruptcy by Kumar and Ravi [68] and Shin et al. [69]. The rough sets are applied to bankruptcy prediction by Dimitras et al. [70], Bioch et al. [71], Ruzgar et al. [72], Shuai and Li [73], and Zaini et al. [74]. Besides these several hybrid techniques are also applied to the bankruptcy prediction problem. These include works by Ahn and Kim [75], Jo et al. [76], Kumar and Ravi [18], Ravi et al. [77], Ryu and Yue [78], Tung et al. [79], Vlachos and Tollias [80], and Wu et al. [81].

The bankruptcy prediction problem has been approached through both statistical- and AI-based techniques. Though AI-based techniques have always produced better prediction results than the classical statistical methods, the quest still remains among the practitioners for superior results catering a wide range of bankruptcy datasets. In this direction, the deep learning networks [82] have emerged as suitable candidate for the bankruptcy prediction problem. Deep learning belongs to the category of Machine Learning algorithms where several layers of nonlinear units of processing are cascaded toward feature extraction and transformation. These algorithms behave in either supervised or unsupervised manner. They learn from different abstraction levels which correspond toward hierarchy of concepts. The hidden layers in the deep network are based on the sets of complicated propositional calculus. Deep learning was first used in algorithms to transform inputs through a number of layers where parameters were iteratively adjusted through training. In the past bankruptcy prediction has never been studied using deep learning networks. The complex HDA structure, viz., FRTDSN-HRB, provides superior bankruptcy prediction performance in terms of accuracy. The learning algorithm uses weight matrices and tensors for parameter estimation whose computational power is increased by incorporating fuzzy rough sets. The integration of HRB enhances the accuracy of prediction of FRTDSN-HRB compared to other models. To achieve comparisons factors' fairness that reduces prediction accuracy is rigorously taken care of through the model. Several experimental results involving important statistical parameters highlight the superiority of FRTDSN-HRB model.

Chapter 4
Bankruptcy Prediction

Bankruptcy prediction [83] is attributed toward predicting bankruptcy and various aspects of distress happening in different companies. Its significance arises when the creditors and investors calculate the likelihood that a company may be bankrupt. The bankruptcy prediction problem is of diverse nature. A possible justification could be the fact that all organizations are of different nature and have limited information which is time not uniform. The quest of the bankruptcy prediction models is not only to look for the explanatory factors but also identify the reasons why a particularly bankruptcy outcome is observed. As a result of this, it is well suited toward the testing of sophisticated and data-intensive prediction approaches. The corporate distress has reached at alarming levels since the end of the last century [1]. With the increase in corporate distress, there was a growth in the number of business failures. There are four generic terms that describe corporate distress, viz., failure, insolvency, default, and bankruptcy, which form the backbone of corporate distress which ultimately leads to bankruptcy:

(a) Failure represents the return rate on capital invested considering allowances with associated risk. On similar investments it is appreciably less than the current rates. A company may be in financial failure for several years, as it is not able to satisfy its present debts.
(b) Insolvency indicates the lack of liquidity and it becomes the important force behind bankruptcy declaration. As a result of this, it incurs more cash. It happens when a company cannot satisfy its financial demands. Bankruptcy appears when the organization's insolvency becomes critical and its total liabilities exceed fair value valuation.
(c) Default is another state that associates itself with distress. It occurs between the debtor company and creditor. A company is not in default as it skips loan or payments of interest. When this problem is not resolved within a specified time, its security appears in default.
(d) Considering failure, insolvency and default bankruptcy is highlighted. A company becomes bankrupt when its total liabilities exceed the total assets of that

© Springer Nature Singapore Pte Ltd. 2017
A. Chaudhuri, S.K. Ghosh, *Bankruptcy Prediction through Soft Computing based Deep Learning Technique*, https://doi.org/10.1007/978-981-10-6683-2_4

firm. The company can also be declared bankrupt by highest prevailing court of law. The court can either declare the organization bankrupt or provide an opportunity toward recovery program. The company participates in a recovery program when its value is more than its liquidation.

During corporate distress the organization's creditors and owners belong to two primary interest groups. These groups are extremely significant in the bankruptcy reorganization process evaluation. The process of reorganization restructures the company in such a way so that the economic stability is achieved.

Let us sketch the major reason behind corporate distress with bankruptcies. Significant amount of research has been done in this direction over the past few decades. Dun and Bradstreet [5] pointed that lack of experience, skewed experience, and incompetence happened to be the primary cause of the company's failures in over 44% of the instances. Another important aspect is the relation between the company's age of an organization and its failure possibility. Dun and Bradstreet argued that more than 50% of all failures occur in companies between the age range of 2–5 years. After 5 years the company organization tends to become stabilized, experienced, and established. As an indirect consequence, they have better access to the capital. The major financial reasons behind an organization's failure are:

(a) Industries: Certain industries are of the sick nature. The companies which perform well initially in these industries are highly likely to fail in the future.
(b) Interest rates: There are companies which fall into position because of high interest rates which they cannot oblige anymore.
(c) Competition: The international competition has gradually intensified the company charges enormously. This scales the advantages in favor of small companies over the big ones. This is because the small companies do business at the price of knife.
(d) Debt to equity: Many companies have their leverage increased. As a result of this, many companies have placed themselves in more obligation situation. In corporate disaster times, these obligations lead to failure.
(e) Deregulation: The deregulation of major industries takes the shape of more competitiveness in the environment.
(f) Formation rates: The higher new business formation rates cause higher company frequency of the failure. These companies have the behavior toward higher failure possibility than the established ones as mentioned earlier.

The financial causes of the organization's failure are more quantifiable statistically. These aspects are highlighted in the deep learning model developed in this research such that it acts as a reliable bankruptcy predictor. Besides the primary interest groups mentioned earlier, the bankruptcy prediction is also important to bond holders and other major players in the financial and legal services. The default risk of a bond is an important factor which influences the bond value. When a company issues a bond and is not capable of meeting the stated obligations, then the issuer has defaulted on the bond. It is very important for the bond holder to figure out the chance of failure of the bond issuer. Bankruptcies are big business for the legal companies. The bankruptcy reorganization processes are highly profitable for these businesses.

The statistical community treats the bankruptcy prediction problem as a binary classification problem [2, 3, 5, 35] quantifying the degree of belief that any particular event will take place. The bankruptcy prediction problem is considered by the machine learning community as the supervised learning technique. Here each instance is the observed dataset that belongs to either of the predefined classes group. The objective is to segregate one class from the other with the minimal error. The investors who wish to evaluate the investment risk always look whether the company is going to be bankrupt in the near future with a certain chance factor. The classification problem input can generally be modeled as financial and other strategic ratio vector. Considering this vector, the classification technique has to assign one of the two possible outputs to the organization, i.e., bankrupt or non-bankrupt. The classification task allocates a new observation B^* to the available v classes which are known a priori. All the classes are mutually exclusive. The allocation procedure depends on the indirect method application considering the feature vectors. Generally it is considered that the correctly labeled data for training and an exact way to classify the observations exists, but it is not feasible to apply always. The indirect classification caters the determination of the financial stress level of any organization because it is not possible to produce a direct assessment. Thus, the financial soundness of a company cannot be ascertained through direct checkup process. Rather it is more suitable to look toward indirect means where organization's financial ratios determine whether it will be bankrupt or not.

A common approach where this strategy is applied relies on the retrieval of the observed financial ratios of number of companies *num* along a window of time *wot* with the financial ratio of each bank denoted by a vector $c_{n,t}$ where the subindex $n \in \{1, num\}$ denotes the bank and the time $t \in \{1, wot\}$ when the data is observed. As the bankruptcies are very rare, the data considered is time-invariant with no dependency. This makes the data independent and identically distributed. A significant amount of research has been performed by considering this approach [4, 5]. It may be noted that by removing the subindex t, the data is effectively considered as of nontemporal nature. The evaluation of company's default probability (*PD*) is required to estimate investment risks. Every company is represented by variables set a which are as predictors like financial ratios and class y that may be $b = -1$ ("successful") or $b = 1$ ("bankrupt"). An unexplored function $f: a \rightarrow b$ is estimated on companies' training set (a_i, b_i); $i = 1, \ldots, n$. The training set considers companies' datasets which are either alive or are bankrupt. Finally, classifier function f is used for calculating *PD* which can be converted into any organization's rating.

Statistical models like option pricing and logit and probit regressions consider that input and output variables relationship may be described a priori. Here the models are described by set of variables. The solution considers the variables estimation on the training dataset. The statistical models give good interpretation of the processes modeled. However, their rigid structure is a cause of concern. The machine learning models like ANN or genetic algorithms (GA) have flexibility in describing data. For the corporate prediction, statistical models have practical significance. The model is generally represented as a probit regression estimation of cumulative default probability covering number of years. The estimation is performed on the univariate models through the nonlinear transformations $h_1, \ldots, h_d$. The original probit model is [5]:

$$Expectation[s_{i,j}|p_{i,j}] = \Theta(\alpha_1 p_{i_1,j} + \ldots + \alpha_d p_{i_d,j}) \qquad (4.1)$$

With this transformation the probit model in Eq. (4.1) is changed into:

$$Expectation[s_{i,j}|p_{i,j}] = \Theta\{\alpha_1 h_1(p_{i_1,j}) + \ldots + \alpha_d h_d(p_{i_d,j})\} \qquad (4.2)$$

In Eq. (4.2), $s_{i,j}$ represents cumulative default probability within the prediction horizon for company i at time t. Though the traditional techniques like probit analysis provide wide spectrum of applicability, it is more often desired to place the methodology based on the statistical learning theory ideas. The classification tool [5] applying the classifying function h from the function set $\mathcal{H}$ is formulated on the expected principle of risk minimization. Here the risk expected is considered as:

$$RiskV(h) = \int \frac{1}{2}|h(p) - s|dP(p,s) \qquad (4.3)$$

This is estimated based on the known distribution function $P(p,s)$. This is very seldom true in practical situations. The distribution is estimated through the training set $(p_i, s_i); i = 1, \ldots, n$. This problem is solved through the empirical risk minimization principle. This minimizes risk over the companies' training set. Here the empirical risk is:

$$\widehat{Risk}(h) = \frac{1}{n} \sum_{i=1}^{n} \frac{1}{2}|h(p_i) - s_i| \qquad (4.4)$$

The empirical risk considers the average loss value considering the training dataset. On the other hand, the expected risk considers the expected loss value under the measure of the true probability. The iid observations' loss is:

$$\frac{1}{2}|h(p) - s| = \begin{cases} 0 & \text{correct classification} \\ 1 & \text{incorrect classification} \end{cases} \qquad (4.5)$$

The expected and the empirical risk minimization solutions are:

$$h_{opt} = \operatorname{argmin}_{h \in \mathcal{H}} R(h) \qquad (4.6)$$

$$\hat{h}_n = \operatorname{argmin}_{h \in \mathcal{H}} \hat{R}(h) \qquad (4.7)$$

The bankruptcy prediction methodology has often been quantified through expected and empirical risk minimization which do not coincide. It is not possible to minimize the expected risk as the distribution of $P(p, s)$ is not known. According to statistical learning theory [84], it becomes possible toward estimating Vapnik-Chervonenkis (VC) bound with probability $1 - \eta$:

$$Risk(h) \leq \widehat{Risk}(h) + \Theta\left(\frac{a}{n}, \frac{\ln(\eta)}{n}\right) \tag{4.8}$$

Considering the indicator function $g(p) = \text{sign}(p^T w + y)$:

$$\Theta\left(\frac{a}{n}, \frac{\ln(\eta)}{n}\right) = \sqrt{\frac{a(\ln(2a/n)) - \ln(\eta/4)}{n}} \tag{4.9}$$

In Eq. (4.9), a represents the VC dimension. The VC dimension of function set $\mathcal{H}$ through d-dimensional space is a if function $h \in \mathcal{H}$ represents a objects $\{p_i \in R^d, i = 1, \ldots, a\}$ in 2^a configurations, and no set $\{p_j \in R^d, j = 1, \ldots, v\}$ exists when $v > a$. VC bound in Eq. (4.9) is a regularized function where VC dimension a controls the complexity of the classifier function. The term $\Theta\left(\frac{a}{n}, \frac{\ln(\eta)}{n}\right)$ gives rise to penalty for classifier function excessive complexity. There always happens a balance between the classification error number on the training dataset and complexity of the classifier function. It is possible to develop a classifier function that makes no errors of classification on the training dataset. It does not even consider its low generalization ability.

Chapter 5
Need for Risk Classification

In most countries a small percentage of companies have been rated for risk classification [5] till date. This rating is attributed because of two reasons. The external rating is an expensive process. Till date most banks have sanctioned loans to small- and medium-sized companies (SME) [5] without any estimation for the associated risks. The banks base their decision-making process on several rough models. The decision to credit is taken up by the loan officer. Learning own's risk is a costly process. The bank's lending process fails to set the correct incentives, making the small- and medium-sized companies to avoid the rating process. The rules revolve around the environment change toward decisions involving lending and borrowing. With the Basel II coming into picture, the companies issue debt securities based on market. This requires rating for which any ordinary company runs for loan from the banks. Here no external rating is available. The banks use internal rating system to sketch the risk class to which the client belongs. The banks are given pressure from both sides by the Basel II. The risk premia is demanded by the banks with respect to the default probability of the specific borrower. The banks have to hold client equity buffers as required by the Basel II.

The Table 5.1 highlights the use case of the individual risk class which is mapped into premiums of risk [39]. Considering the small European companies, 1-year probability of default for 0.17% results in 4% spread. Here lenders' mapping differs if the company type or the country changes where the bank is stationed. The future loan pricing follows the basic rule. The risk premium charged by the bank grows as the company's risk increases.

The Basel committee [5] specifies the buffer size which is determined by risk weight function with coefficient of solvability as 10%. The probabilities of default probabilities are transformed into risk weights by this function. The switching from Basel I to Basel II through the capital requirement changes per loan unit is highlighted in Table 5.2. The weights depend also on the type of loan and the annual turnover other than the basic risk components such as PD, maturity, and loss given default (LGD) risk. The Table 5.2 refers to retail loan and considers the borrower's turnover as ten million euro. The loan provision costs are affected by the

© Springer Nature Singapore Pte Ltd. 2017
A. Chaudhuri, S.K. Ghosh, *Bankruptcy Prediction through Soft Computing based Deep Learning Technique*, https://doi.org/10.1007/978-981-10-6683-2_5

Table 5.1 The rating grades and risk premia

Rating class (S &P)	1-year PD (%)	Risk premia (%)
AAA	0.02	0.80
AA	0.04–0.06	1.25
A⁺	0.07	1.75
A	0.10	2.00
A⁻	0.17	2.75
BBB	0.17–0.44	3.50
BB	0.69–1.98	4.75
B⁺	3.55	6.00
B	8.00	7.75
B⁻	19.00	9.25
CCC	>19	11.25
CC		12.75
C		14.90
D		16.25

Table 5.2 The rating class and Basel I and Basel II capital requirements; the last column figures are determined for the retail loan with ten million euros turnover with 5-year maturity

Rating class (S &P)	1-year PD (%)	Capital requirements (%) (Basel I)	Capital requirements (%) (Basel II)
AAA	0.02	10.00	0.69
AA	0.04–0.06	10.00	0.96–1.50
A⁺	0.07	10.00	1.70
A	0.10	10.00	2.17
A⁻	0.17	10.00	2.86
BBB	0.17–0.44	10.00	3.17–5.38
BB	0.69–1.98	10.00	6.70–10.48
B⁺	3.55	10.00	12.96
B	8.00	10.00	17.86
B⁻	19.00	10.00	24.96
CCC	>19	10.00	>24.96
CC		10.00	
C		10.00	
D		10.00	

lock-in of bank's equity. The borrower directly handles these costs. When the company requires external finance, it is affected by the Basel II. The company's rating has deeper economic impact on banks and the company itself when the risk premium and credit costs are determined through the default risk. In the Basel II the right rating method choice is very critical. To avoid large magnitude friction, the employed method should satisfy certain conditions. On the other hand, rating procedure should place the misclassifications amount at the lowest level. It should be straightforward as possible. If the borrower employs it, some guidance should be provided to improve his own financial rating.

Chapter 6
Experimental Framework: Bankruptcy Prediction Using Soft Computing Based Deep Learning Technique

The experimental framework consists of predicting bankruptcy through soft computing based deep learning technique. Deep learning has evolved a promising machine learning technique in past few years [82]. It is deep structured learning and concerned with ANN study containing more than one hidden layer. It is based on composition of several layers with nonlinear units toward feature extraction and corresponding transformation. Here each preceding layer provides input to successive layer. Deep learning algorithms are executed in either supervised or unsupervised manner. These algorithms learn from multiple representation levels corresponding to several abstraction levels. Deep learning has been successfully applied toward several categories of pattern recognition and computer vision problems with considerable success.

Basically the deep classification architecture is constructed using simplified ANN modules. Here each module consists of input, output single nonlinear hidden layers. It has been coined as the deep convex network [82]. The weights in upper layer are learned by structuring it mathematically as convex optimization problem. The weights in lower layers in every block are initialized as Boltzmann machine. Later is coined as deep stacking network (DSN) [31]. Deep architecture here is based on the stacked generalization philosophy. It recognizes the fact that the lower-layer weights learn for better accuracy in classification tasks.

The deep learning technique for the bankruptcy prediction problem revolves around the hierarchical deep architecture which integrates deep learning model with structured hierarchical Bayesian model [85]. The hierarchical deep architecture is based on tensor deep stacking networks (TDSN) which is enriched through fuzzy rough sets leading to fuzzy rough tensor deep stacking networks (FRTDSN). FRTDSN significantly improves the DSN architecture. The information regarding the higher-order statistics is injected into FRTDSN. This is achieved by bilinear mapping through hidden representations toward third-order tensors. FRTDSN has the similar linear-nonlinear shape which is present with DSN. Another significant feature is the representation of the hidden units in FRTDSN which helps to tackle the large bankruptcy datasets considered in this work [5]. The similar interleaved

© Springer Nature Singapore Pte Ltd. 2017
A. Chaudhuri, S.K. Ghosh, *Bankruptcy Prediction through Soft Computing based Deep Learning Technique*, https://doi.org/10.1007/978-981-10-6683-2_6

linear and nonlinear layer nature is adapted from DSN. Upper layers with the closed-form solution allow effective parallel training. The smaller size of the hidden layers brings no factorization for the tensor weights in FRTDSN. It also optimizes the least squares objective and achieves considerable scalability and parallelization. FRTDSN parallelizes all the training and evaluation calculations and scales well to larger training sets using exclusively CPU-based cluster. The fuzzy rough sets in FRTDSN handle vagueness and impreciseness with corporate bankruptcy datasets. Next the rough sets [86] are incorporated in structured hierarchical Bayesian model such that hierarchical rough Bayesian (HRB) model is evolved. The rough sets in HRB identify and recognize the common patterns in bankruptcy data hierarchically based on the approximation present in the classification space. They also take care of the incompleteness present in the bankruptcy datasets. The sub-models in HRB integrate to form the hierarchical model which results in posterior distribution that is used for parameter estimation. FRTDSN is then integrated with HRB to form the compound FRTDSN-HRB model. HRB enhances the overall prediction power of FRTDSN-HRB model. The schematic diagram of overall process is represented in Fig. 6.1. The deep stacking networks (DSN) are initially introduced. This is followed by FRTDSN. Next the mathematical framework of HRB model is presented. Finally the compound FRTDSN-HRB is explained.

6.1 Deep Stacking Networks

DSN are deep convex networks consisting of ANN blocks which define the module [31]. Its learning process is achieved in a parallel weight manner. The training is performed through supervised and block-wise manner with no back propagation [62]. DSN blocks consist of straightforward learning modules that are stacked toward the formation of the deep network. There is upper-layer weight matrix **UM** which connects nonlinear hidden layer **hd** to linear layer **ya**. The lower-layer weight matrix **WM** connects input and hidden layers. The target vectors **tv** are **TV** columns. The input data vectors **xv** are arranged as the columns of **XV**. The matrix of hidden units is denoted by $\mathbf{HT} = \sigma(\mathbf{WM}^T\mathbf{XV})$, where the lower-layer weights **WM** are assumed to be known and the function σ performs elementwise logistic sigmoid operation:

$$\sigma(x) = \frac{1}{1 + e^{-x}} \tag{6.1}$$

The upper-layer weight matrix **UM** learning process is:

$$\min_{\mathbf{UM}^T} f = \left\| \mathbf{UM}^T\mathbf{HT} - \mathbf{TV} \right\|_F^2 \tag{6.2}$$

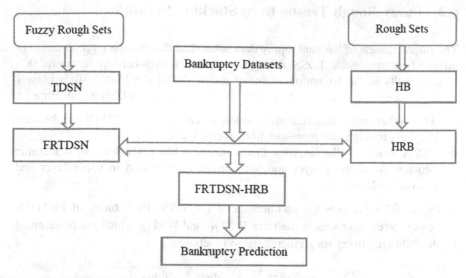

Fig. 6.1 The FRTDSN-HRB for bankruptcy prediction

Equation (6.2) has a closed-form solution. The bottom block **XV** has the input. For the DSN higher blocks, output representations from prior blocks are concatenated with input data. The optimization of the lower-layer weight matrix WM in DSN is achieved through the accelerated gradient descent [62] which minimizes the squared error objective in Eq. (6.2). The target vectors **tv** are arranged as vector **TV**. The solution from objective function and gradient derivation is:

$$\nabla \mathbf{w}f = \mathbf{XV}\left[\mathbf{HT}^{T*}\left(\mathbf{1} - \mathbf{HT}^{T}\right)^{*}\mathbf{\Theta}\right] \tag{6.3}$$

In Eq. (6.3) **1** is ones matrix with * as multiplication operation with:

$$\mathbf{\Theta} = 2\mathbf{HT}\left(\mathbf{HT} \cdot \mathbf{TV}^{T}\right)\left(\mathbf{TV} \cdot \mathbf{HT}\right) - \mathbf{TV}^{T}\left(\mathbf{TV} \cdot \mathbf{HT}\right) \tag{6.4}$$

In order to train the DSN block, **WM** is iteratively updated through the gradient in Eq. (6.4). It considers the optimal weight **UM**. After **WM** is calculated, **UM** is estimated. DSN never discovers transformed feature representations. DSN is thus easily parallelizable with simple and optimized network weights. For purely discriminative tasks, DSN works better than deep belief networks [31]. The label class estimate is continuous valued function. The decision to classify is done at top block. The DSN lower blocks have output vector not used toward decision. It is rather used to concatenate with original input vector fed directly to upper block.

6.2 Fuzzy Rough Tensor Deep Stacking Networks

The impreciseness of the bankruptcy data is handled through the representation of different parameters of TDSN through fuzzy rough membership functions [87] which results in the formation of fuzzy rough TSDN (FRTSDN). It is closely related to deep stacking networks (DSN). FRTDSN improves DSN architecture as:

(a) The higher-order statistics information is enforced into TDSN via bilinear mapping through two representations which are hidden.
(b) TDSN retains similar linear-nonlinear structure like DSN. It arranges learning problem from lower layer and non-convex optimization to upper layer and convex subproblem.

Figure 6.2 represents the architecture of FRTDSN. Each block of FRTDSN possesses lower-layer weight matrices $\widetilde{\mathbf{WM}}_{(1)}$ and $\widetilde{\mathbf{WM}}_{(2)}$ which are represented by the following fuzzy rough membership function:

$$\alpha_i(p) = \begin{cases} 1 - \left(\dfrac{\sum_{i=1}^{H}\mu_{FC_i}(p)\tau_{C_c}^i}{\sum_i \mu_{FC_i}(p)}\right)\sqrt{\dfrac{\|\text{dist}_{i+}^2\| - \|\text{dist}_{i+}^2\|}{\|\text{dist}_{i+}^2\| + \|\text{dist}_{i+}^2\| + \varepsilon}} & \text{if } \text{dist}_{i+}^2 > t \\ 1 - \left(\dfrac{\sum_{i=1}^{H}\mu_{FC_i}(p)\tau_{C_c}^i}{\sum_i \mu_{FC_i}(p)}\right)\sqrt{\dfrac{\|\text{dist}_{i-}^2\| - \|\text{dist}_{i-}^2\|}{\|\text{dist}_{i-}^2\| + \|\text{dist}_{i-}^2\| + \varepsilon}} & \text{if } \text{dist}_{i-}^2 < t \end{cases}$$

$$(6.5)$$

In Eq. (6.5), dist_{i+}^2 and dist_{i-}^2 represent the maximum and minimum distances, respectively, with respect to threshold t between the weight matrices $\widetilde{\mathbf{WM}}_{(1)}$ and $\widetilde{\mathbf{WM}}_{(2)}$. The term $(\cdot)$ in Eq. (6.5) is valid as $(\exists i)\mu_{FC_i}(p) > 0$ with $\varepsilon > 0$ and $\alpha_i(p) \neq 0$.

The input layer $\mathbf{XT}$ is connected with sigmoidal hidden layers $\widetilde{\mathbf{HT}}_{(1)}$ and $\widetilde{\mathbf{HT}}_{(2)}$ branches shown in Fig. 6.2. FRTDSN block contains a three-way upper-layer weight tensor $\widetilde{\mathcal{VT}}$. FRTDSN architecture performs bankruptcy prediction with good accuracy. Its effectiveness is further improved when it is interfaced with HRB as discussed in Sect. 6.4. Each FRTDSN block has two hidden representations. It combines them in a bilinear way to yield the predictions. FRTDSN customizes the single-block structure by taking the linear map from hidden to output.

At the same time, it retains its modeling as well as the estimation properties. The mapping in FRTDSN takes the form $\widetilde{\mathbb{R}}^{P_1} \times \widetilde{\mathbb{R}}^{P_2} \to \widetilde{\mathbb{R}}^V$ represented through fuzzy rough numbers in accordance with Eq. (6.5).

The first step in FRTDSN maps an input vector $\mathbf{xt} \in \widetilde{\mathbb{R}}^I$ to two parallel hidden branches of representations, viz., $\widetilde{\mathbf{ht}}_{(1)} \in \widetilde{\mathbb{R}}^{P_1}$ and $\widetilde{\mathbf{ht}}_{(2)} \in \widetilde{\mathbb{R}}^{P_2}$. Each hidden

Fig. 6.2 FRTDSN architecture with stacking blocks

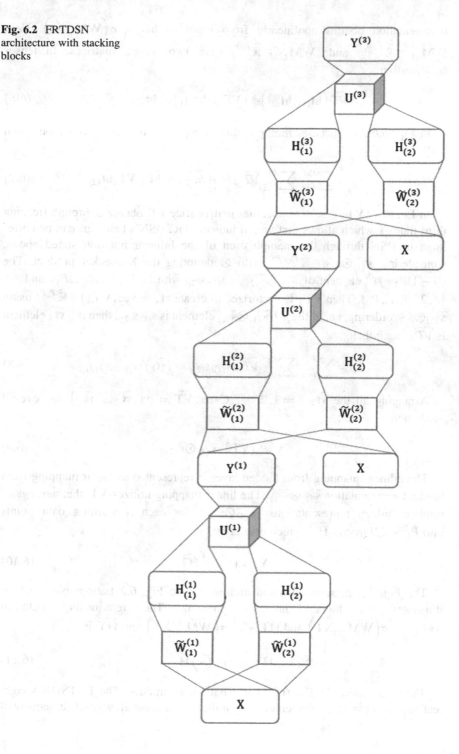

representation obtains nonlinearly from input as $\widetilde{\mathbf{ht}}_{(j)} = \sigma\left(\widetilde{\mathbf{WM}}_{(j)}^T \mathbf{xt}\right)$. Here $\widetilde{\mathbf{WM}}_{(1)} \in \widetilde{\mathbb{R}}^{I \times P_1}$ and $\widetilde{\mathbf{WM}}_{(2)} \in \widetilde{\mathbb{R}}^{I \times P_2}$ are two weight matrices. In tensor specification:

$$\widetilde{\mathcal{VT}}\left(\widetilde{\mathbf{ht}}_{(1)}, \widetilde{\mathbf{ht}}_{(2)}\right) \triangleq \left(\widetilde{\mathcal{VT}} \times_1 \widetilde{\mathbf{ht}}_{(1)}\right) \times_2 \widetilde{\mathbf{ht}}_{(2)} = \widetilde{\mathbf{y}} \tag{6.6}$$

In Eq. (6.6), $\times_i$ specifies multiplication along i^{th} dimension tensor mode such that:

$$\tilde{y}_k = \sum_{i=1}^{P_1} \sum_{j=1}^{P_2} \widetilde{\mathcal{VT}}_{ijk} \widetilde{ht}_{(1)i} \widetilde{ht}_{(2)j} = \widetilde{\mathbf{ht}}_{(1)}^T \widetilde{\mathbf{VT}}_k \widetilde{\mathbf{ht}}_{(2)} \tag{6.7}$$

In Eq. (6.7) $\widetilde{\mathbf{VT}}_k \in \widetilde{\mathbb{R}}^{P_1 \times P_2}$ specifies matrix slice $\widetilde{\mathcal{VT}}$ obtained through freezing third index k which allows first varied indices. FRTDSN's behavior can be correlated to DSN through the manipulation of the bilinear notation stated above. Considering $\tilde{\mathbf{s}}_{(1)} \otimes \tilde{\mathbf{s}}_{(2)} \in \widetilde{\mathbb{R}}^{P_1 \times P_2}$ with $\otimes$ denoting the Kronecker product. The $((i-1)P_2+j)^{th}$ element of $\tilde{\mathbf{s}}_{(1)} \otimes \tilde{\mathbf{s}}_{(2)}$ is $s_{(1)i}s_{(2)j}$ with $i \in \{1, 2, \ldots, P_1\}$ and $j \in \{1, 2, \ldots, P_2\}$. Then $\widetilde{\mathbf{VT}}_k$ is vectorized to create $\widetilde{\mathbf{vt}}_k = \text{vec}\left(\widetilde{\mathbf{VT}}_k\right) \in \widetilde{\mathbb{R}}^{P_1 P_2}$ using $\tilde{\mathbf{s}}_{(1)} \otimes \tilde{\mathbf{s}}_{(2)}$ ordering, i.e., if the pth $\tilde{\mathbf{s}}_{(1)} \otimes \tilde{\mathbf{s}}_{(2)}$ element is $s_{(1)i}s_{(2)j}$, then p^{th} $\widetilde{\mathbf{vt}}_k$ element is $\widetilde{\mathcal{VT}}_{ijk}$ such that:

$$\tilde{y}_k = \sum_{i=1}^{P_1} \sum_{j=1}^{P_2} \widetilde{\mathcal{VT}}_{ijk} s_{(1)i} s_{(2)j} = \left(\widetilde{\mathbf{vt}}_k\right)^T \tilde{\mathbf{s}}_{(1)} \otimes \tilde{\mathbf{s}}_{(2)} \tag{6.8}$$

Arranging all the $\widetilde{\mathbf{vt}}_k, k = 1, 2, \ldots, C$ as $\widetilde{\mathbf{VT}} = \left[\widetilde{\mathbf{vt}}_1 \widetilde{\mathbf{vt}}_2 \ldots \widetilde{\mathbf{vt}}_C\right]$ the overall prediction becomes:

$$\tilde{\mathbf{y}} = \left(\widetilde{\mathbf{VT}}\right)^T \tilde{\mathbf{s}}_{(1)} \otimes \tilde{\mathbf{s}}_{(2)} \tag{6.9}$$

The bilinear mapping from hidden layer is represented as linear mapping from implicit representation $\tilde{\mathbf{s}}_{(1)} \otimes \tilde{\mathbf{s}}_{(2)}$. The linear mapping utilizes $\widetilde{\mathbf{VT}}$ that aggregates implicit hidden representations $\tilde{\mathbf{s}}_{(1)} \otimes \tilde{\mathbf{s}}_{(2)}$ for each N training data points into $P_1 P_2 \times N$ matrix $\widetilde{\mathbf{HT}}$ which results in:

$$\widetilde{\mathbf{Y}} = \left(\widetilde{\mathbf{VT}}\right)^T \widetilde{\mathbf{HT}} \tag{6.10}$$

The Fig. 6.3 presents identical architecture to Fig. 6.2 bottom block which illustrates the hidden layers expansion. The relationship between $\widetilde{\mathbf{HT}}_{(1)} = \sigma\left(\widetilde{\mathbf{WM}}_{(1)}^T \mathbf{XT}\right)$ and $\widetilde{\mathbf{HT}}_{(2)} = \sigma\left(\widetilde{\mathbf{WM}}_{(2)}^T \mathbf{XT}\right)$ and $\widetilde{\mathbf{HT}}$ is:

$$\widetilde{\mathbf{HT}} = \tilde{\mathbf{H}}_1 \odot \tilde{\mathbf{H}}_2 \tag{6.11}$$

The O operation in Eq. (6.11) is Khatri-Rao product. The FRTSDN weight learning process is implemented in parallel or sequential way. The sequential

Fig. 6.3 The architecture to bottom block of Fig. 6.2 with tensor unfolded into large matrix

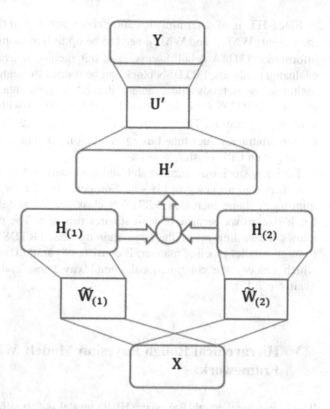

approach is first discussed followed by the parallel implementation. As the architectures in Figs. 6.2 and 6.3 are equivalent, the second layer weight learning is similar to the same least squares problem.

6.2.1 Learning FRTDSN Weights – Sequential and Parallel Implementation

In the sequential implementation, the problem is approached through the Tikhonov regularized optimization problem where the target matrix $\widetilde{\mathbf{TM}}$ is trained as:

$$\min_{\widetilde{\mathbf{VT}}^T} f = \left\| \widetilde{\mathbf{TM}} - \widetilde{\mathbf{VT}}^T \widetilde{\mathbf{HT}} \right\|_F^2 + \lambda \left\| \widetilde{\mathbf{VT}} \right\|_F^2 \tag{6.12}$$

Equation (6.12) has the closed-form solution. With the closed-form solution, learning process is more effective through coupling of the lower and upper weight matrices. Upper-layer weights in FRTDSN are deterministically calculated through lower-layer weights. As a result of this, they need not be learned separately and independently. There are constraints available in FRTDSN.

Since $\widetilde{HT}$ is of deterministic nature corresponding to the lower-layer weights, the weights $\widetilde{WM}_{(1)}$ and $\widetilde{WM}_{(2)}$ need to be optimized using only first-order oracle information [31]. A detail discussion of this method is available at [5]. Using the evaluated gradients, FRTDSN block can be trained through available second-order optimization methods and gradient descent implementations [5]. The training process of FRTDSN requires around 10–17 iterations with about 8 gradient evaluations per iteration. The weight matrices $\widetilde{WM}_{(1)}$ with $\widetilde{WM}_{(2)}$ are initialized as certain arbitrary values tuned using validation set. The training is parallelized by running it on CPU cluster.

Basically stochastic mini-batch training is used in deep learning training. There is reduction in accuracy of classification performance for gradient methods when mini-batch shape increases. FRTDSN classification accuracy enhances as mini-batch size grows because of least squares problem. The parallel training method allows the scaling up of the large training sets. FRTDSN is trained in parallel through parallel pipeline manner. It consists of parallelizing the matrix operations which reduces the computational complexity considerably. Further details are available at [5].

6.3 Hierarchical Rough Bayesian Model: Mathematical Framework

The hierarchical rough Bayesian (HRB) model is formalized hierarchically using rough set based Bayesian model which is crafted through probability based rough sets [2] and Bayesian statistics [5]. The Bayesian approach is the natural process toward aggregating information sources with uncertainty management. The data is adopted from multiple sources. The model is developed through stochastic parameters with an expert opinion. The predictive distributions are based on quantities of interest which conditioned through observations. The hierarchical model is grown through conditional thinking. The prima face here is on the number of uncertainty sources. The joint distribution is represented as the product of the conditionals. The decomposition choice is based on the knowledge about the process and the necessary assumptions for simplification. The conditional models have a straightforward representation than full joint models. The hierarchical model accounts toward the individual and group level variations when the group level coefficients are estimated. Through this they borrow strength across the groups which minimize small sample size effects present in certain groups. The random effects absorb the present variations which are not related with the fixed effects. This helps to achieve potentially lower bias for fixed effect estimates. The random effects also take care of the unmeasured variations. The hierarchical model always works well by taking care of the relevant group variations. In order to provide the mathematical formulation of HRB, a basic review of probabilistic rough sets is presented first followed by the classification and estimation tasks provided by rough Bayesian model.

6.3.1 Decision Theoretic Rough Sets

The brief review of rough sets is provided here. To begin with, consider an equivalence relation $EV \subseteq UV \times UV$ on UV. The tuple $aprs = (UV, EV)$ depicts the approximation space. EV grows the partition of UV by UV/EV. Universe of discourse UV is divided into the following five disjoint regions with $CV \subseteq UV$ [86] as:

(a) Positive region $POSR(CV)$
(b) Positive boundary region $BNDR^+(CV)$
(c) Boundary region $BNDR(CV)$
(d) Negative boundary region $BNDR^-(CV)$
(e) Negative region $NEGR(CV)$

The stated five regions for an object $xv \in UV$ are expressed mathematically as:

$$POSR(CV) = \{xv \in UV | [xv] \subseteq CV\} \tag{6.13}$$

$$BNDR^+(CV) = \{xv \in UV | [xv] \cap CV \neq \varnothing \wedge [xv] \subseteq CV\} \tag{6.14}$$

$$BNDR(CV) = \{xv \in UV | [xv] \cap CV \neq \varnothing \wedge [xv] \nsubseteq CV\} \tag{6.15}$$

$$BNDR^-(CV) = \{xv \in UV | [xv] \cap CV = \varnothing \wedge [xv] \nsubseteq CV\} \tag{6.16}$$

$$NEGR(CV) = \{xv \in UV | [xv] \cap CV = \varnothing\} \tag{6.17}$$

It can well be placed with a degree of certainty that object $xv \in POSR$ (CV) belongs to CV and vice versa for object $xv \in NEGR(CV)$. It is quite uncertain to argue that whether or not an object $BNDR^+(CV), BNDR(CV),$ and $BNDR^-(CV)$ belongs to CV. This considers the overlap degrees between the equivalence classes and the approximation sets. The conditional probability that the object belongs to CV such that object is in $[xv]$ is estimated as:

$$Prob(CV | [xv]) = \frac{|CV \cap [xv]|}{|[xv]|} \tag{6.18}$$

In Eq. (6.18) $|\cdot|$ is the set cardinality. Accordingly the five regions stated earlier can be equivalently represented as:

$$POSR(CV) = \{xv \in UV \mid Prob(CV\mid[xv]) = 1\} \tag{6.19}$$

$$BNDR^+(CV) = \{xv \in UV \mid 0 \le Prob(CV\mid[xv]) < 1\} \tag{6.20}$$

$$BNDR(CV) = \{xv \in UV \mid 0 < Prob(CV\mid[xv]) < 1\} \tag{6.21}$$

$$BNDR^-(CV) = \{xv \in UV \mid 0 < Prob(CV\mid[xv]) \le 1\} \tag{6.22}$$

$$NEGR(CV) = \{xv \in UV \mid Prob(CV\mid[xv]) = 0\} \tag{6.23}$$

Equations (6.19), (6.20), (6.21), (6.22), and (6.23) are defined through values 0 and 1. These equations represent qualitative values for $Prob(CV\mid[xv])$. The magnitude is not considered here. The results of the rough sets are parameterized through certain probabilistic approximations. The values 0 and 1 in Eqs. (6.19), (6.20), (6.21), (6.22), and (6.23) can be replaced by threshold a and b such that $a < b$. The tuple (a, b) has the positive, positive boundary, boundary, negative boundary, and negative regions specified through probability as:

$$POSR_{(a,b)}(CV) = \{xv \in UV \mid Prob(CV\mid[xv]) \ge a\} \tag{6.24}$$

$$BNDR^+_{(a,b)}(CV) = \{xv \in UV \mid b \le Prob(CV\mid[xv]) < a\} \tag{6.25}$$

$$BNDR_{(a,b)}(CV) = \{xv \in UV \mid b < Prob(CV\mid[xv]) < a\} \tag{6.26}$$

$$BNDR^-_{(a,b)}(CV) = \{xv \in UV \mid b < Prob(CV\mid[xv]) \le a\} \tag{6.27}$$

$$NEGR_{(a,b)}(CV) = \{xv \in UV \mid Prob(CV\mid[xv]) \le b\} \tag{6.28}$$

The above stated five probabilistic regions give rise to five-way decisions [88, 89, 90, 91, 92]. The object xv as member of CV is accepted if the probability is greater than a. The object xv as member of CV is rejected if probability is less than b. The object xv as member of CV is neither accepted nor rejected if the probability is between a and b. Here deferment decision is taken. The threshold values a and b are interpreted as the cost parameters of the classification involved. These values are evaluated through reducing classification risk. For interested readers further insights on rough sets are available in [86].

6.3.2 Classification Based on Rough Bayes Model

Now classification based on the rough Bayes model is highlighted. It is not always easy to derive the conditional probabilities from data. The Bayes theorem is the commonly applied method to calculate such values:

$$Prob(CV|[xv]) = \frac{Prob(CV)Prob([xv]|CV)}{Prob([xv])} \tag{6.29}$$

Again $Prob([xv])$ is represented as:

$$Prob([xv]) = Prob([xv]|CV)Prob(CV) + Prob([xv]|CV^c)Prob(CV^c) \tag{6.30}$$

In Eq. (6.30) $Prob(CV|[xv])$ is the posteriori probability of class CV given $[xv]$, $Prob(CV)$ is the apriori probability of class CV, and $Prob([xv]|CV)$ is the likelihood of $[xv]$ with respect to CV. The probability $Prob([xv])$ in Eq. (6.30) can be eliminated by taking odds form of Bayes theorem which is given as:

$$Odd(Prob(CV|[xv])) = \frac{Prob(CV|[xv])}{Prob(CV^c[xv])} = \frac{Prob([xv]|CV)}{Prob([xv]|CV^c)} \cdot \frac{Prob(CV)}{Prob(CV^c)}$$

$$= \frac{Prob([xv]|CV)}{Prob([xv]|CV^c)} Odd(Prob(CV)) \tag{6.31}$$

The probability threshold value is considered as threshold on odds. The positive region is represented as:

$$Prob(CV|[xv]) \geq a \Leftrightarrow \frac{Prob(CV|[xv])}{Prob(CV^c[xv])}$$

$$\geq \frac{a}{1-a} \Leftrightarrow \frac{Prob([xv]|CV)}{Prob([xv]|CV^c)} \cdot \frac{Prob(CV)}{Prob(CV^c)} \geq \frac{a}{1-a} \tag{6.32}$$

Considering logarithms to Eq. (6.32) results in:

$$\log \frac{Prob([xv]|CV)}{Prob([xv]|CV^c)} + \log \frac{Prob(CV)}{Prob(CV^c)} \geq \log \frac{a}{1-a} \tag{6.33}$$

Identical statements are also derived for negative and boundary regions. The five regions are represented as:

$$POSR_{(a',b')}^{BR}(CV) = \{xv \in UV| \log \frac{Prob([xv]|CV)}{Prob([xv]|CV^c)} \geq a'\} \tag{6.34}$$

$$BNDR_{(a,b)}^{BR^+}(CV) = \{xv \in UV| b' \leq \log \frac{Prob([xv]|CV)}{Prob([xv]|CV^c)} < a'\} \tag{6.35}$$

$$BNDR_{(a',b')}^{BR}(CV) = \{xv \in UV| \ b' < \log \frac{Prob([xv]|CV)}{Prob([xv]|CV^c)} < a'\} \qquad (6.36)$$

$$BNDR_{(a,b)}^{BR^-}(CV) = \{xv \in UV| \ b' < \log \frac{Prob([xv]|CV)}{Prob([xv]|CV^c)} \leq a'\} \qquad (6.37)$$

$$NEGR_{(a',b')}^{BR}(CV) = \{xv \in UV| \ \log \frac{Prob([xv]|CV)}{Prob([xv]|CV^c)} \leq b'\} \qquad (6.38)$$

In Eqs. (6.34), (6.35), (6.36), (6.37), and (6.38), a and b are represented as:

$$a' = \log \frac{Prob(CV^c)}{Prob(CV)} + \log \frac{a}{1-a} \qquad (6.39)$$

$$b' = \log \frac{Prob(CV^c)}{Prob(CV)} + \log \frac{b}{1-b} \qquad (6.40)$$

This interpretation simplifies calculation by eliminating $Prob([xv])$. Interested readers can refer [86] for further know-how on rough sets.

6.3.3 Rough Bayesian Model for Estimating Probabilities

The naive rough Bayesian model allows conditional probability estimation with respect to naive Bayesian classification. Information table is represented as [88, 89, 90, 91, 92]:

$$SV = (UV, Bt, \{V_b|b \in Bt\}, \{I_b|b \in Bt\}) \qquad (6.41)$$

Here UV is the universe, Bt represents the attribute set, V_b denotes values toward $b \in Bt$, and $I_b : UV \rightarrow V_b$ is the information function. The Bayesian interpretation of regions based on Eq. (6.41) considers the following expression:

$$Prob(Descp[xv]|CV) = Prob(v_1, \ldots \ldots, v_n|CV) = \prod_{i=1}^{n} Prob(v_i|CV) \qquad (6.42)$$

$$Prob(Descp[xv]|CV^c) = Prob(v_1, \ldots \ldots, v_n|CV^c) = \prod_{i=1}^{n} Prob(v_i|CV^c) \qquad (6.43)$$

Equations (6.42) and (6.43) are reexpressed as:

$$\log \frac{Prob(Descp[xv]|CV)}{Prob(Descp[xv]|CV^c)} \geq \log \frac{Prob(CV)}{Prob(CV^c)} + \log \frac{a}{1-a}$$

$$\Leftrightarrow \sum_{i=1}^{n} \log \frac{Prob(v_i|CV)}{Prob(v_i|CV^c)} \geq \log \frac{Prob(CV)}{Prob(CV^c)} + \log \frac{a}{1-a}$$

(6.44)

Here the probability terms $Prob(CV)$ and $Prob(v_i|CV)$ are estimated as:

$$Prob(CV) = \frac{|CV|}{|UV|}$$

(6.45)

$$Prob(v_i|CV) = \frac{|st(b_i, v_i) \cap CV|}{|CV|}$$

(6.46)

Here $st(b_i, v_i)$ is defined through $st(b_i, v_i) = \{xv \in UV | I_{b_i}(xv) = v_i\}$. Similarly the probability terms $Prob(CV^c)$ and $Prob(v_i|CV^c)$ are estimated. The Eqs. (6.34), (6.35), (6.36), (6.37), and (6.38) are rewritten as:

$$POSR_{(a',b')}^{BR}(CV) = \left\{ xv \in UV \Big| \sum_{i=1}^{n} \log \frac{Prob(v_i|CV)}{Prob(v_i|CV^c)} \geq a' \right\}$$

(6.47)

$$BNDR_{(a,b)}^{BR^+}(CV) = \left\{ xv \in UV \Big| b' \leq \sum_{i=1}^{n} \log \frac{Prob(v_i|CV)}{Prob(v_i|CV^c)} < a' \right\}$$

(6.48)

$$BNDR_{(a',b')}^{BR}(CV) = \left\{ xv \in UV \Big| b' < \sum_{i=1}^{n} \log \frac{Prob(v_i|CV)}{Prob(v_i|CV^c)} < a' \right\}$$

(6.49)

$$BNDR_{(a,b)}^{BR^-}(CV) = \left\{ xv \in UV \Big| b' < \sum_{i=1}^{n} \log \frac{Prob(v_i|CV)}{Prob(v_i|CV^c)} \leq a' \right\}$$

(6.50)

$$NEGR_{(a',b')}^{BR}(CV) = \left\{ xv \in UV \Big| b' < \sum_{i=1}^{n} \log \frac{Prob(v_i|CV)}{Prob(v_i|CV^c)} \leq a' \right\}$$

(6.51)

6.3.4 Hierarchical Rough Bayesian Model

Based on the mathematical formulations presented in previous subsections, HRB model [85] is now presented here. It is represented through multiple levels in hierarchical form. The parameters' estimation from posterior distribution is performed through using Bayesian statistics. Sub-models are integrated such that the hierarchical model is evolved. Bayes' theorem combines with the observed data and takes care of the uncertainty present. This leads to the posterior distribution with a requirement of additional evidence on the a priori distribution. The Bayesian statistics treats parameters as random variables. It uses subjective information through which the assumptions are validated on the stated parameters. This model is more robust such that the posterior distribution has lesser sensitivity against the hierarchical priors. The hierarchical model works effectively with multiparameter problems toward the formation of the computational framework. In this process the rough Bayesian hierarchical model uses two vital aspects toward deriving the posterior distribution [85]:

(a) Hyperparameter which forms the parameter of a priori distribution. It distinguishes itself from the models' parameters with respect to the system concerned for analysis. Here either a single value may be considered or it may iterate toward the probability distribution on the hyperparameter.
(b) Hyperprior which forms the distribution of the a priori distribution. They come in picture when conjugate priors are used. This becomes abstract and is taken away from the actual problem.

To verify abovementioned components toward rough Bayesian hierarchical structure, consider random variable Y with parameters α and 1 as the mean and variance, respectively, such that $Y \mid \alpha \sim N(\alpha, 1)$. The parameter α has prior distribution which is represented through normal distribution such that $Y \mid \vartheta \sim N(\vartheta, 1)$. The parameter ϑ is modeled through standard normal distribution $N(0, 1)$. The hyperparameter distribution is $N(0, 1)$ and shows the hyperprior distribution. The distribution of Y changes when another parameter is added such that $Y \mid \alpha, \vartheta \sim N(\vartheta, 1)$. When another stage is present, then ϑ follows normal distribution with mean δ and variance ρ such that $\vartheta \sim N(\delta, \rho)$. Here δ and ρ are the hyperparameters and they are distributed as hyperprior distributions.

Consider y_j as an observation and α_j as the parameter which governs through the data generation process for y_j. It is assumed that the parameters $\alpha_1, \ldots \ldots, \alpha_j$ are generated when exchange is performed from a common population having the distribution through the hyperparameter ω. The parameters α and ω represent the random variables. The hierarchical rough Bayesian model is drawn through the stages as highlighted below. This is a three-stage model which can be extended to n-stage model.

(a) Stage I: $y_j | \alpha_j, \omega \sim Prob(y_j | \alpha_j, \omega.)$
(b) Stage II: $\alpha_j | \omega \sim Prob(\alpha_j | \omega)$
(c) Stage III: $\omega \sim Prob(\omega)$

The likelihood as represented in the Stage I is $Prob(y_j | \alpha_j, \omega)$ with $Prob(\alpha_j, \omega)$ as the a priori distribution. The likelihood depends on ω only through α_j. The a priori distribution from Stage I is:

$$Prob(\alpha_j, \omega) = Prob(\alpha_j | \omega)Prob(\omega) \qquad (6.52)$$

The distribution ω is the hyperparameter with hyperprior distribution $Prob(\omega)$. The posteriori distribution now becomes:

$$Prob(\omega, \alpha_j | y) \propto Prob(y_j | \alpha_j, \omega) Prob(\alpha_j | \omega) \tag{6.53}$$

$$Prob(\omega, \alpha_j | y) \propto Prob(y_j | \alpha_j) Prob(\alpha_j, \omega) \tag{6.54}$$

6.4 Compound FRTDSN-HRB Model

Considering the mathematical formulation of FRTDSN and HRB in Sects. 6.2 and 6.3, the compound FRTDSN-HRB model is developed here. The motivation toward the development of this mathematical framework is adopted from [5]. The compound FRTDSN-HRB model is schematically represented in the figure below. An undirected model is considered that is defined through joint distribution $Prob(\mathbf{s}, \mathbf{v}^{(1)}, \mathbf{v}^{(2)}, \mathbf{v}^{(3)})$. The concerned information is given as $Prob(\mathbf{s}, \mathbf{v}^{(1)}, \mathbf{v}^{(2)} | \mathbf{v}^{(3)})$ along with a priori term $Prob(\mathbf{v}^{(3)})$. The parameter $\mathbf{s} \in \{0, 1\}^H$ represents the visible units sets and sequence of hidden units $\mathbf{v}^{(1)} \in \{0, 1\}^{J_1}$, $\mathbf{v}^{(2)} \in \{0, 1\}^{J_2}$, and $\mathbf{v}^{(3)} \in \{0, 1\}^{J_3}$. The variation bound is rewritten with ϑ as the vector parameters:

$$\log Prob(\mathbf{s}) \geq \sum_{\mathbf{v}^{(1)} \ \mathbf{v}^{(2)} \ \mathbf{v}^{(3)}} P(\mathbf{v}|\mathbf{s}; \vartheta) \log Prob\left(\mathbf{s}, \mathbf{v}^{(1)}, \mathbf{v}^{(2)} | \mathbf{v}^{(3)}\right) + \mathcal{H}(P)$$
$$+ \sum_{\mathbf{v}^{(3)}} P\left(\mathbf{v}^{(3)}|\mathbf{s}; \vartheta\right) \log Prob\left(\mathbf{v}^{(3)}\right) \tag{6.55}$$

This decomposition takes care of greedy recursive pretraining where conditional probability $Prob(\mathbf{s}, \mathbf{v}^{(1)}, \mathbf{v}^{(2)} | \mathbf{v}^{(3)})$ is preserved. However lower bound variation in Eq. (6.55) is maximized. This maximization replaces $Prob(\mathbf{v}^{(3)})$ by a prior that closely approximates the conditional posterior $P(\mathbf{v}^{(3)} | \mathbf{s})$. Instead of considering an additional undirected layer to $Prob(\mathbf{v}^{(3)})$, a prior is placed over $\mathbf{v}^{(3)}$ that allows category hierarchy learning and useful class representations. The term $Prob(\mathbf{s}, \mathbf{v}^{(1)}, \mathbf{v}^{(2)} | \mathbf{v}^{(3)})$ represents conditional FRTDSN:

$$Prob\left(\mathbf{s}, \mathbf{v}^{(1)}, \mathbf{v}^{(2)} | \mathbf{v}^{(3)}\right)$$
$$= \frac{1}{Z(\tilde{\psi}, \mathbf{v}^{(3)})} \exp\left(\sum_{ij} \tilde{V}_{ij}^{(1)} s_i w_j^{(1)} + \sum_{jl} \tilde{V}_{jl}^{(2)} v_j^{(1)} v_l^{(2)} + \sum_{lk} \tilde{V}_{lk}^{(3)} v_l^{(2)} v_k^{(3)}\right) \tag{6.56}$$

Equation (6.56) represents the two-layer FRTDSN with bias terms as $\mathbf{v}^{(3)}$ states. $\tilde{\psi} = \left\{\tilde{\mathbf{V}}^{(1)}, \tilde{\mathbf{V}}^{(2)}, \tilde{\mathbf{V}}^{(3)}\right\}$ represents fuzzy rough visible-to-hidden and hidden-to-hidden terms. In the compound FRTDSN-HRB model, HRB is used as the prior considering FRTDSN activities with respect to high-level features.

It has been assumed that the model is highlighted through two-level partition $\mathbf{p} = \{\mathbf{p}^s, \mathbf{p}^b\}$ defining a fixed two-level tree hierarchy. The standard FRTDSN assumes fixed hierarchy for parameter sharing. Nonparametric nested Chinese restaurant prior is placed above $\mathbf{p}$. The situation is treated as a process where customers land to restaurant with unbounded tables. Here nth customer takes table k:

$$Prob(p_n = k|p_1 \ldots p_{n-1}) = \begin{cases} \dfrac{n^k}{n-1+\eta}, n^k > 0 \\ \dfrac{\eta}{n-1+\eta}, ow \end{cases} \qquad (6.57)$$

In Eq. (6.57), n^k is number of earlier customers at table k and η is concentration parameter. The corresponding inferences regarding the model parameters at different hierarchies are performed through Markov chain Monte Carlo algorithm. On aggregating likelihood term with Chinese restaurant process prior, posterior above category assignment is:

$$Prob\left(\mathbf{p}_n|\boldsymbol{\omega}_n, \mathbf{p}_{-n}, \boldsymbol{\rho}^{(1)}\right) \propto Prob\left(\boldsymbol{\omega}_n|\boldsymbol{\rho}^{(1)}, \mathbf{p}_n\right) Prob(\mathbf{p}_n|\mathbf{p}_{-n}) \qquad (6.58)$$

In Eq. (6.58) $\mathbf{p}_{-n}$ represents the variables $\mathbf{p}$ for all the observations except n. The conditioning based on the assignments y_{in} and $\mathbf{v}_n^{(2)}$ depends on the multinomial unit $\mathbf{v}_n^{(3)}$ states toward each input n. They are sampled through the Gibbs conditionals:

$$Prob\left(\mathbf{v}_{in}^{(3)}| \mathbf{v}_n^{(2)}, \mathbf{v}_{-in}^{(3)}, \mathbf{y}_n\right) \propto Prob\left(\mathbf{v}_n^{(2)}| \mathbf{v}_n^{(3)}\right) Prob\left(\mathbf{v}_{in}^{(3)}|\mathbf{y}_{in}\right) \qquad (6.59)$$

In Eq. (6.59) first term is logistic functions product such that:

$$Prob\left(\mathbf{v}_n^{(2)}| \mathbf{v}_n^{(3)}\right) = \prod_j Prob\left(\mathbf{v}_{jn}^{(2)}| \mathbf{v}_n^{(3)}\right) \qquad (6.60)$$

$$Prob\left(v_j^{(2)} = 1| \mathbf{v}_n^{(3)}\right) = \frac{1}{1 + \exp\left(-\sum_k \tilde{V}_{jk}^{(3)} v_k^{(3)}\right)} \qquad (6.61)$$

The conditioning based on the $\mathbf{v}^{(3)}$ states further fine-tunes the low-level FRTSDN parameters $\tilde{\boldsymbol{\psi}} = \left\{\tilde{\mathbf{V}}^{(1)}, \tilde{\mathbf{V}}^{(2)}, \tilde{\mathbf{V}}^{(3)}\right\}$. This is achieved by approximate maximum likelihood learning toward the conditional FRTSDN. The low-level FRTSDN features are fine-tuned which significantly improves the model's performance. Now in order to look toward the predictions, a test input $\mathbf{s}_t$ is considered from which quick inference can be performed regarding the approximate posterior over $\mathbf{v}_t^{(3)}$. This uses the mean field along with the full Gibbs sampler to teach approximate samples from posterior considering category assignments. In practice, faster inference fixes the topics ω_t. Along with this the marginal likelihood is approximated such that $\mathbf{v}_t^{(3)}$ belongs to $\mathbf{p}_t$ category. This assumes that the sample-specific process is well approximated by the class-specific process. Hence, instead of aggregating the sample-specific process, an approximation is computed through integration of the assignments y_{in}:

$$Prob\left(\mathbf{v}_t^{(3)} | \mathbf{p}_t, Y^{(1)}, \omega \right) = \int Prob\left(\mathbf{v}_t^{(3)} | \omega, Y_t \right) Prob\left(Y_t | Y_{\mathbf{p}_t}^{(1)} \right) dY_t$$

$$\approx Prob\left(\mathbf{v}_t^{(3)} | \omega, Y_{\mathbf{p}_t}^{(1)} \right) \tag{6.62}$$

On combining the likelihood term with Chinese restaurant prior $Prob(\mathbf{p}_t | \mathbf{p}_{-t})$, there arises an opportunity to efficiently infer the approximate posterior considering the category assignments. The approximate posterior calculation takes minimal time which is critical for the bankruptcy prediction task to be performed.

Chapter 7
Datasets Used

Now we present the different bankruptcy datasets which are used to perform several experiments. For this research work, we have considered the following bankruptcy datasets. These datasets are considerably restructured to highlight the success of compound FRTSDN-HRB presented in Chap. 6:

(a) Korean construction companies [32]: The financial data of Korean construction companies is adapted and applied to the proposed prediction model. The data is taken from the companies' financial statements for 10-year period. The financial data from NICE DnB contains all the construction companies' data in Korea where they are classified as bankrupt and normal. The bankrupt companies' data considered were taken from the period 2007–2016. These companies achieved the bankrupt status during this period. The normal companies are not placed in the state of bankruptcy as on December 2016. There are 1686 bankrupt and 30,489 normal companies considered. The data 1 year after the bankruptcy is taken considering the bankrupt companies. This helps to effectively observe the bankruptcy level after 1-year period. The 2015 financial data is used for the other companies. Now with respect to the accumulated data, the following parameters as shown in Table 7.1 are developed and used for the experiments.

Each variable is taken as ratio such that they are applied with respect to the size of the capital size or company sales. According to the classification by size of the capital, the companies are segregated as small, medium, and big companies. Tables 7.2 and 7.3 highlight the descriptive statistics of the model parameters considering all construction companies in Korea and their correlation matrix. With respect to the capital size, the construction companies are classified as small, medium, and big companies. The small Korean construction companies have capital worth below 700 million won. The capital of the medium Korean construction companies are placed in the range of 700 million to 100 billion won. The capital of the big Korean construction companies are more than 100 billion

© Springer Nature Singapore Pte Ltd. 2017
A. Chaudhuri, S.K. Ghosh, *Bankruptcy Prediction through Soft Computing based Deep Learning Technique*, https://doi.org/10.1007/978-981-10-6683-2_7

Table 7.1 The bankruptcy variables and their significance

Variables	Significance
EBIT/TA	Refers to the earnings before interest and taxes to the total assets
EBT/CAP	Refers to the earnings before taxes to the capital
WC/TA	Refers to the working capital to the total assets
WC/S	Refers to the working capital to the sales
CA/TA	Refers to the current assets to the total assets
CA/CL	Refers to the current assets to the current liabilities
C/TA	Refers to the cash to the total assets
C/CL	Refers to the cash to the current liabilities
$\log_e$TA	Refers to the value of natural logarithm of the total assets
S/CAP	Refers to the sales to the capital
S/CA	Refers to the sales to the current assets
S/TA	Refers to the sales to the total assets

Table 7.2 The descriptive statistics of the parameters of all the Korean construction companies

Variables	Mean	Median	Standard deviation
WC/S	−14.09	−0.04	310.04
C/CL	0.69	0.05	5.89
S/CA	4.55	3.38	7.04
EBIT/TA	−0.16	0.06	0.99
CA/TA	0.65	0.65	0.35
WC/TA	−0.35	−0.05	6.89
S/TA	1.78	1.35	1.86
EBT/CAP	−1.89	0.14	77.79
S/CAP	121.55	10.86	4875.35
$\log_e$TA	10.48	10.48	1.96
C/TA	0.08	0.05	0.20
CA/CL	3.69	1.20	18.86

won. The bankrupt companies' ratio with respect to the capital size is depicted in Table 7.4. There are some big construction companies with relatively high bankruptcy ratio. There are a large number of small construction companies with relatively low bankruptcy ratio. The large construction companies have the high bankruptcy ratio such that the overall bankruptcy loss is high.

(b) American and European nonfinancial companies [33]: The financial data of American and European nonfinancial companies is adapted and applied to the proposed prediction model. Here the financial data is taken from 1000 US and 350 European nonfinancial companies. The European dataset has the companies from the European Union states with Germany having 50 companies, France having 50 companies, and rest of the companies belonging to other states. The United Kingdom has 55 companies. The two datasets are taken up separately as the companies with financial ratios outside the United States do not have directly comparable statistics. The outside US companies differ in

Table 7.3 The correlation matrix on the parameters of all the Korean construction companies

S/CAP	EBT/CAP	0.89
CA/CL	C/CL	0.79
S/TA	S/CA	0.69
C/TA	C/CL	0.48
C/TA	CA/TA	0.48
S/TA	CA/TA	0.38
EBT/CAP	WC/S	0.35
C/TA	S/TA	0.25
EBIT/TA	S/CA	0.20
CA/CL	C/TA	0.20
CA/CL	CA/TA	0.19
WC/TA	S/CA	−0.69
WC/TA	EBIT/TA	−0.64
S/TA	WC/TA	−0.48
$\log_e$TA	S/TA	−0.38
C/TA	$\log_e$TA	−0.35
CA/TA	S/CA	−0.35
$\log_e$TA	CA/TA	−0.27
$\log_e$TA	C/CL	−0.27
CA/CL	$\log_e$TA	−0.27
$\log_e$TA	S/CA	−0.21
CA/CL	S/CA	−0.10

Table 7.4 The bankruptcy ratio with respect to the capital size

Size of capital (in won)	Bankrupt companies	Normal companies	Bankruptcy ratio
< 700 million	286	10,896	2.62%
700 million – 100 billion	1169	18,306	6.38%
> 100 billion	231	1287	17.95%
Total	1686	30,489	5.53%

goodwill treatment, asset valuation practices, contingent liabilities reporting, accounting techniques, etc. The country risks are not considered. For each variable mean values are calculated over the years 2007–2016. The 10-year average follows the rating through cycle process adopted through rating agencies in order to achieve stability and minimize the business cycle effect. This longer-term perspective is implemented through 10-year averages of relevant financial ratios. The rating stability has been satisfied mathematically. When predicting bankruptcy the bankruptcy ratings show a high autocorrelation and the key input variable is the previous years' ratings. The S&P's rating agency assigns the ratings with 2017 as the target classes. The ratings are expressed through a single scale where the rating agencies take into consideration several diverse national considerations. The parameters considered describe the companies into two categories as business position and financial indicators. The former describes the company through factors such as industry risk, size, character, management skills, etc. The company size is presented through measuring market capitalization, assets, equity, cash flow, etc. The company's ability to pay off its debts is determined through company size. A correlation is developed for company size with diversification and market power. The company's reputation is a difficult measure. This factor is determined through information about insiders and institutional holdings. The industry risk represents the company's sensitivity in a specific industry or market to external business factors. The reputation and industry risk have only been considered to certain degree. The financial indicators are also considered in the corporate bankruptcy rating process. The financial indicators are divided as profitability ratios, activity ratios, liquidity ratios, leverage ratios, and market value ratios. The profitability ratios depict asset management influence as well as company's financing and liquidity on profit. The profitability ratios include absolute profit size, return on total asset effect, return on equity, return on sales, operating margin, and net margin. The activity ratios present asset management effectiveness. The asset management influence on the company's bankruptcy rating is indirect because asset management belongs to the financial decision-making areas. The current ratio represents the liquidity ratios. The other parameters such as quick ratio and cash ratio are also used. The leverage ratios are depicted through total debts to total assets. The company's capability to pay off debt is assessed from the generated profit. The market value ratios reflect past company activity and direction toward the future. The correlation between stock returns with market index, high/low stock price, and dividend yield is also considered important for bankruptcy prediction.

Table 7.5 shows the input variables list which are used to cover the US and European companies. The input variables chosen for the experiments are presented in Table 7.6. The US dataset contains 81 input variables obtained from the value line and the S&P's databases. The European dataset covers only subset of the input variables represented in italics. The input variables are divided into nine categories as company size, corporate reputation, profitability ratios, activity ratios, asset structure, business situation, liquidity ratios, leverage ratios, and market value ratios. A feature selection step selects subset of parameters from the sets presented in Table 7.6. The companies are classified as nine output rating classes. The principal component analysis closely assesses the data nature. Fourteen principal components with eigenvalues greater than 1 are considered from the original set of 81 variables (the US dataset) and 43 variables (the European dataset). The first principal component presents 50.20% and 20.38% of total variance, respectively. The US dataset represents input variables from several categories correlated with the companies' size. The second component presents the company's capital market position. The first component for European companies has the label capital market position. The second component shows the companies size.

Table 7.5 The bankruptcy prediction input variables considered

Company size		Business situation	
TA	Total assets	*ETR*	*Effective tax rate*
TC	*Total capital*	S gr	Growth in sales last year
S	*Sales (last year)*	S exp	Expected growth in S (next 5 years)
TS	*12-month trailing sales*	SGAE	SG&A expenditures
CF	*Cash flow*	**Liquidity ratios**	
E	Equity	CR	Current ratio
EV	Enterprise value	CaR	Cash ratio
FV	*Firm value*	*Cash/FV*	*Cash to firm value*
CE	*Capital expenditures*	*Cash*	*Cash*
SC	Size class	NCWC	Noncash working capital
MC	*Market capitalization*	**Leverage ratios**	
TV	Trading volume	*BV/E*	*Book value to equity*
NS	No. of shares outstanding	*BD/TC*	*Book debt to total capital*
Corporate reputation		*EV/TC*	*Enterprise value to total capital*
IH	*Shares held by mutual funds*	EV/BV	Enterprise value to book value
lnH	Shares held by insiders	MC/TD	Market capitalization to debt
Profitability ratios		*TD*	*Total debt*
EBIT	Earnings before interest and taxes	CF/TD	*Cash flow to total debt*
EAT	Earnings after taxes	MD/E	*Market debt to equity*
NI	*Net income*	MD/TC	*Market debt to total capital*
TNI	12-month trailing NI	NG	Net gearing
NM	*Net margin*	*MD/ EBITDA*	*Market debt to EBITDA*
OM	*Operating margin*	**Market value ratios**	
ROA	Return on total assets	*P var*	*3-year stock price variation*
ROE	*Return on equity*	*Beta*	*Beta regression coefficient (3 years)*
ROC	*Return on capital*	VLB	Value line beta
EBITDA	*EBIT increased by depreciation and amortization*	*Cor*	*The correlation of stock returns with market index*
EV/ EBITDA	*Enterprise value to EBITDA*		
HiLo	*High/low stock price*		
EV/ EBIT	*Enterprise value to EBIT*	Div	Dividends
RE/TA	Retained earnings to total assets	*Div/P*	*Dividends to stock price*
Activity ratios		EPS	Earnings per share
EV/S	*Enterprise value to sales*	EPS gr	Growth in earnings per share (last 5 years)
NCWC gr	*Growth in NCWC*	*EPS exp*	*Expected growth in earnings per share (next 5 years)*
EV/TS	Enterprise value to trailing sales	P/CF	Stock price to cash flow
S/NW	Sales to net worth	*P/E*	*Stock price to earnings*

(continued)

Table 7.5 (continued)

Company size		Business situation	
S/TA	Sales to total assets	TP/E	12-month trailing stock price to earnings
OR/TA	Operating revenue to total assets	FP/E	Forward stock price to earnings
WC/S	Working capital to sales	*PEG*	*Stock price to earnings to EPS growth*
Cash/S	Cash to sales	*PBV*	*Price-to-book value ratio*
NCWC/S	Noncash working capital to sales	RE	Retained earnings
Asset structure		*RR*	*Reinvestment rate*
FA/TA	Fixed assets to total assets	*PR*	*Payout ratio*
IA/TA	Intangible assets to total assets	*PS*	*Stock price to sales*
WC/TA	Working capital to total assets	*P*	*Stock price*
Dep	Depreciation		

Table 7.6 The bankruptcy prediction potential input variables

Input variables	Input variables
Current ratio	Retained earnings/total assets
Net margin	Market to book value
Total liabilities	Long term debts/total capital
Return on equity	Sales/fixed assets
Earnings	Market equity value
Net income	Return on capital
Size class	Intangible assets/total assets
Stock returns	Mutual funds
Interest coverage	Total debts/total assets
Total assets	Return on total assets
Total debts/total assets	Operating margin
Cash flow	KMV Merton probability
Short term debts	Beta regression coefficient
Quick ratio	Cash ratio
Dividend yield	High/low stock price
Market capitalization	Tax rate

Table 7.7 The bankruptcy variables and their significance

Attributes	Significance
Industrial risk	The risk which company bears from the industrial impact
Management risk	The risk which company bears from the management
Financial flexibility	The financial flexibility of the company
Credibility	The company's credibility to its creditors
Competitiveness	The company's overall competitiveness in the market
Operating risk	The risk involved in company's operation

(c) UCI Machine Learning Repository Bankruptcy database [34]: The bankruptcy
    database from the UCI Machine Learning Repository is applied to proposed
    prediction model. The database was created by J. Uthayakumar and
    M. Nadarajan in September 2013. The dataset is considerably restructured for
    performing the several experiments to validate the credibility of the compound
    FRTSDN-HRB. The database has originally 175 instances with six attributes
    which correspond to the qualitative bankruptcy parameters. The database does
    not have any missing attribute values. These instances are increased to 1000 [5]
    through the data generator which adapts the behavior of the original dataset.
    The new dataset has 400 bankrupts and 600 normal companies. The different
    attributes of the dataset are briefly highlighted in Table 7.7.

Chapter 8
Experimental Results

Now the results toward predicting bankruptcy are highlighted here by the proposed compound FRTDSN-HRB using the (a) Korean construction companies, (b) American and European nonfinancial companies' datasets, and (c) UCI Machine Learning Repository bankruptcy database. A comparative study of FRTDSN-HRB with FSVM, MFSVM, Bayesian, hazard, mixed logit, and rough Bayesian models is also presented. The models are implemented through Matlab 9.1 on PC with Intel Core i7 processor, the configuration of which is 6.40 GHz, 128 GB RAM, and 16 MB cache. The experimental results are presented as cutoff point, Type I and Type II errors, optimal cutoff point, and randomly selected samples spread across several full and mid-business cycles.

8.1 Cutoff Point, Type I and Type II Errors: Korean Construction Companies

When the fitted probability of the company is higher than cutoff point, it is considered as bankrupt and otherwise. When the company is bankrupt and is placed in the non-bankrupt class, then error is Type I or else it is Type II. In order to highlight the relationship between cutoff point, Type I and Type II errors, the total sample is segregated as the training and holdout samples. There are 1686 bankrupt and 30,489 normal companies in the training sample. The training sample evaluates prior probabilities for all the techniques. The error types are calculated through the holdout sample which is obtained through classification. The training sample works on the prior probabilities toward all the models, and holdout sample calculates two types of error. Considering the number of companies in the class, the error rate is computed as the number of misclassified companies. The Type I error increases when the cutoff point moves forward. The cutoff point grows as the Type II error goes down. The rate of Type I error is below one when the probability obtained

© Springer Nature Singapore Pte Ltd. 2017

A. Chaudhuri, S.K. Ghosh, *Bankruptcy Prediction through Soft Computing based Deep Learning Technique*, https://doi.org/10.1007/978-981-10-6683-2_8

Table 8.1 Predictive results with different cutoff points (Korean companies)

Cutoff point	FRTDSN-HRB			FSVM		
	Type I	Type II	Type I + II	Type I	Type II	Type I + II
50%	0.3628	0.0006	0.3634	0.4886	0.0148	0.5034
0.50%	0.0201	0.2754	0.2955	0.0086	0.5596	0.5682
3.80%	0.2069	0.0369	0.2438	0.1069	0.2169	0.3238
	MFSVM			Bayesian		
Cutoff point	Type I	Type II	Type I + II	Type I	Type II	Type I + II
50%	0.4097	0.0127	0.4224	0.3754	0.0796	0.4550
0.50%	0.0086	0.4896	0.4982	0.0269	0.5364	0.5633
3.80%	0.1779	0.2499	0.4278	0.1164	0.2164	0.3328
	Hazard			Mixed Logit		
Cutoff point	Type I	Type II	Type I + II	Type I	Type II	Type I + II
50%	0.8928	0.0007	0.8935	0.4286	0.0148	0.4434
0.50%	0.0804	0.2548	0.3352	0.0089	0.5796	0.5885
3.80%	0.3575	0.0364	0.3939	0.1072	0.2189	0.3261
	Rough Bayesian					
Cutoff point	Type I		Type II		Type I + II	
50%	0.4886		0.0124		0.5010	
0.50%	0.0069		0.4897		0.4966	
3.80%	0.1272		0.2165		0.3437	

using Bayesian model becomes zero or higher than one. The cutoff point is considered as one even when the Type II error rate can go over zero. To evaluate the bankruptcy models, the accuracy of classification is applied to the method of validation. To choose the cutoff point of 50%, there are some important methods when it is difficult to incorporate the prior probability and the costs. The 0.50% cutoff rate of industry failure assumes as the sample probability which is the group membership's a priori probability.

The sum of Type I and Type II errors is minimized through the 3.8% cutoff point. Table 8.1 shows the results based on the several cutoff points. The rate of Type I or Type II errors is considering through each model. The sum of Type I and Type II errors is given by the Type I + Type II. As the cutoff point is taken as 50%, the Bayesian model achieves better performance than others when validation is considered through Type I error. As Type I + Type II errors are used, then FRTDSN-HRB, FSVM, MFSVM, hazard, mixed logit, and rough Bayesian models achieve superior performance with respect to the cutoff points 0.50% and 3.8%. However these results do not convey the models' true quality. There are certain drawbacks. When the validation method represents the sum of two errors, there is spurious of equal costs with respect to the misclassification. The Type II error cost is 30 times lower than the Type I error. It happens when Type I error occurs and the total principle is lost by the creditors. This is with respect to the opportunity cost which results through the Type II error. In each group the numbers of companies differences are ignored in this analysis. The number of normal companies is greater than the bankrupt companies.

8.2 Cutoff Point, Type I and Type II Errors: American and European Nonfinancial Companies

In analogy with the Korean construction companies' dataset, similar analysis is performed with the American and European nonfinancial companies. The company is classified as bankrupt if its probability is higher than cutoff point. If company is bankrupt and the classification results show it as normal, then the error is Type I; otherwise, it is Type II. In order to represent the association among cutoff point, Type I and Type II errors, the total sample is randomly and equally grouped into training and holdout samples. The US training sample consists of 800 normal and 200 bankrupt companies. The European training sample has 300 normal and 50 bankrupt companies. For all the models, the training sample calculates prior probabilities and holdout sample performs the classification to arrive at two error types. The results are shown in Tables 8.2 and 8.3 with respect to several cutoff points. The error rate is computed as number of companies which are wrongly classified considering the number of companies with respect to the whole class. The accuracy of classification is applied to validation method in order to have a comparative analysis of the prediction models. The results are shown in Tables 8.2 and 8.3 with respect to different cutoff points.

8.3 Cutoff Point, Type I and Type II Errors: UCI Machine Learning Repository Bankruptcy Database

Now the analysis for the UCI Machine Learning bankruptcy database is presented. As in the previous case, the company is placed in the bankrupt class when the cutoff point is less than its fitted probability. The Type I and Type II errors hold for bankrupt company on similar lines stated earlier. The association between cutoff point, Type I and Type II errors, is highlighted when total sample is randomly and equally grouped into training and holdout samples. Training sample consists of 600 normal and 400 bankrupt companies. Considering all the models, the training sample calculates prior probabilities and holdout sample performs the classification to calculate two error types. The results are shown in Table 8.4 with respect to several cutoff points. The error rate is computed as the number of companies which are misclassified with respect to the companies in the whole group. The classification accuracy is applied to the validation method to compare the bankruptcy models.

Table 8.2 Predictive results with different cutoff points (US companies)

Cutoff point	FRTDSN-HRB			FSVM		
	Type I	Type II	Type I + II	Type I	Type II	Type I + II
50%	0.3528	0.0001	0.3529	0.4886	0.0148	0.5034
0.50%	0.0600	0.2748	0.3348	0.0269	0.5096	0.5365
3.80%	0.3044	0.0348	0.3392	0.0650	0.1969	0.2619
Cutoff point	MFSVM			Bayesian		
	Type I	Type II	Type I + II	Type I	Type II	Type I + II
50%	0.3096	0.0124	0.3220	0.3650	0.0696	0.4346
0.50%	0.0089	0.4886	0.4975	0.0057	0.4860	0.4917
3.80%	0.0976	0.2186	0.3162	0.1060	0.1964	0.3024
Cutoff point	Hazard			Mixed logit		
	Type I	Type II	Type I + II	Type I	Type II	Type I + II
50%	0.7528	0.0001	0.7529	0.4086	0.0248	0.4334
0.50%	0.0501	0.2548	0.3049	0.0069	0.5496	0.5565
3.80%	0.3470	0.0269	0.3739	0.1069	0.2079	0.3148
Cutoff point	Rough Bayesian					
	Type I		Type II			Type I + II
50%	0.4089		0.0224			0.4313
0.50%	0.0168		0.4896			0.5064
3.80%	0.1872		0.2065			0.3937

Table 8.3 Predictive results with different cutoff points (European companies)

Cutoff point	FRTDSN-HRB			FSVM		
	Type I	Type II	Type I + II	Type I	Type II	Type I + II
50%	0.3096	0.0121	0.3217	0.3450	0.0596	0.4046
0.50%	0.0086	0.1086	0.1172	0.0096	0.4048	0.4144
3.80%	0.0875	0.1986	0.2861	0.1055	0.1969	0.3024
Cutoff point	MFSVM			Bayesian		
	Type I	Type II	Type I + II	Type I	Type II	Type I + II
50%	0.3454	0.0699	0.4153	0.3660	0.0696	0.4356
0.50%	0.0148	0.4050	0.4198	0.0191	0.4169	0.4387
3.80%	0.1054	0.1860	0.2914	0.1054	0.1964	0.3018
Cutoff point	Hazard			Mixed logit		
	Type I	Type II	Type I + II	Type I	Type II	Type I + II
50%	0.7828	0.0002	0.7830	0.3686	0.0219	0.3905
0.50%	0.0601	0.2144	0.2745	0.0069	0.5096	0.5165
3.80%	0.3270	0.0160	0.3430	0.1060	0.2077	0.3137
Cutoff point	Rough Bayesian					
	Type I		Type II			Type I + II
50%	0.4086		0.0221			0.4307
0.50%	0.0164		0.4896			0.5060
3.80%	0.1969		0.2040			0.4009

Table 8.4 Predictive results with different cutoff points (UCI Machine Learning Repository database)

Cutoff point	FRTDSN-HRB			FSVM		
	Type I	Type II	Type I + II	Type I	Type II	Type I + II
50%	0.3428	0.0006	0.3434	0.4896	0.0148	0.5044
0.50%	0.0101	0.2754	0.2855	0.0086	0.5596	0.5682
3.80%	0.1972	0.0369	0.2341	0.1969	0.2169	0.4138
Cutoff point	MFSVM			Bayesian		
	Type I	Type II	Type I + II	Type I	Type II	Type I + II
50%	0.4096	0.0127	0.4223	0.3755	0.0798	0.4553
0.50%	0.0086	0.4896	0.4982	0.0169	0.5364	0.5533
3.80%	0.1979	0.2499	0.4478	0.1064	0.2164	0.3228
Cutoff point	Hazard			Mixed logit		
	Type I	Type II	Type I + II	Type I	Type II	Type I + II
50%	0.8928	0.0007	0.8935	0.4886	0.0148	0.5034
0.50%	0.0804	0.2550	0.3354	0.0089	0.5796	0.5885
3.80%	0.3679	0.0364	0.4043	0.1072	0.2189	0.3261
Cutoff point	Rough Bayesian					
		Type I		Type II		Type I + II
50%		0.4886		0.0124		0.5010
0.50%		0.0069		0.4897		0.4966
3.80%		0.1969		0.2165		0.4134

8.4   Optimal Cutoff Point: Korean Construction Companies

This section highlights the optimal cutoff point analysis toward Korean construction companies. The correct cutoff point reduces misclassification cost as:

$$\min_{\alpha} \text{Cost} = \sum_{i=1}^{n} \left[\text{Cost}_{I,i} I(\widehat{\text{Prob}}_i \leq \alpha) \right]^{y_i} \left[\text{Cost}_{II,i} I(\widehat{\text{Prob}}_i > \alpha) \right]^{(1-y_i)} \quad (8.72)$$

Here Cost is total misclassification cost, $\text{Cost}_{I,i}$ and $\text{Cost}_{II,i}$ are the Type I and Type II error cost toward company i, α represents cutoff point, $\widehat{\text{Prob}}_i$ represents bankruptcy probability toward the company i, y_i is observed status toward the company i, and $I(\cdot)$ represents the indicator function. However the computational time is increased through this estimation. Equation (8.72) provides simplified total cost minimization:

$$\min_{\alpha} \text{Cost} = \text{Cost}_I \text{Prob}_I(\alpha) \text{Rate}_I + \text{Cost}_{II} \text{Prob}_{II}(\alpha) \text{Rate}_{II} \quad (8.73)$$

Here, $Prob_I$ and $Prob_{II}$ are Type I and Type II error rates, α is cutoff point function, and $Rate_I$ and $Rate_{II}$ are normal and bankrupt company rates'. The optimal cutoff point is unknown beforehand toward the holdout sample. The optimal cutoff point proxy can be determined.

The cutoff point can also be estimated using training sample. To determine the empirical cutoff point using training sample in holdout sample, random selection sample is executed 30 times. Training sample evaluates a priori probabilities. It also computes empirical cutoff point. Holdout sample generates the prediction results. For this purpose three other cutoff points 0.50%, 3.8%, and 50% are selected. Paired sample t tests are performed under each cutoff points' pair. Table 8.5 gives results using various cutoff points. The first column in the table has the ratios of cost of Type I to Type II errors. A robust check is performed through several ratio specifications. Here mathematical optimal cutoff point calculated with training sample is the best proxy toward true optimal cutoff point for holdout sample. This is because it exceeds the specifications of Type I costs above Type II costs through minimum cost of misclassification. Such results hold good considering all the prediction models. The second best cutoff point is 0.50%. This is not proper considering the low ratio of Type I to Type II cost. This happens because most companies are placed which reduces Type I error cost while simultaneously increasing Type II error cost. The 50% cutoff point is utilized as the Type I error and Type II error costs are considered. However mathematical results point that it produces greater misclassification cost when two cost types are assumed as identical.

8.5   Optimal Cutoff Point: American and European Nonfinancial Companies

Here the optimal cutoff point analysis for the American and European nonfinancial companies is presented. The appropriate cutoff point that reduces misclassification cost is calculated using Eq. (8.72). As discussed in Sect. 8.4, the cutoff point is estimated using training sample. The training sample calculates the a priori probabilities and empirical cutoff point. Prediction results are generated by the holdout sample. The cutoff points considered are 0.50%, 3.8%, and 50% for the American and European nonfinancial companies' datasets. Paired sample t tests are performed for each pair of cutoff points. The results using various cutoff points are given in Tables 8.6 and 8.7.

Table 8.5 Random selection and test results (Korean companies)

$\frac{Cost_I}{Cost_{II}}$; Cost; α	FRTDSN-HRB				FSVM			
	0.50%	3.8%	50%	Optimal	0.50%	3.8%	50%	Optimal
1	0.1936	0.0354	0.0486	0.0436*	0.2460	0.0554*	0.0686	0.0648
10	0.2196	0.3669	0.6965	0.1969*	0.2596	0.4072	0.7465	0.2469*
20	0.2540*	0.7255	1.4355	0.3086*	0.3848*	0.7855	1.5455	0.3486
35	0.3148*	1.1968	2.5531	0.3543	0.4048	1.3267	2.6734	0.4079*
50	0.4172*	1.8921	3.6196	0.3655*	0.4872*	1.9621	3.8696	0.4555*
75	0.5586	2.8672	5.4069	0.5177*	0.6186*	2.9672	5.6969	0.6077*
100	0.6981*	3.4348	7.7286	0.4075*	0.7484	3.6040	7.8986	0.6975*
$\frac{Cost_I}{Cost_{II}}$; Cost; α	MFSVM				Bayesian			
	0.50%	3.8%	50%	Optimal	0.50%	3.8%	50%	Optimal
1	0.2036	0.0455	0.0586	0.0648*	0.5274	0.2332	0.0913	0.0776*
10	0.2496	0.4870	0.7265	0.2169	0.5438	0.3228	0.4596	0.2977*
20	0.2948*	0.7755	1.5255	0.3186*	0.5620	0.4324*	0.8687	0.4348*
35	0.3548*	1.3169	2.6131	0.4048	0.5893*	0.5718*	1.4824	0.6289
50	0.4372	1.9221	3.6996	0.4355*	0.6165	0.7211	2.0962	0.5772*
75	0.5586	2.9172	5.4369	0.5577*	0.6621*	0.9702	3.1181	0.6536*
100	0.7281*	3.5540	7.7986	0.4375*	0.7076*	1.2192	4.1434	0.7169*
$\frac{Cost_I}{Cost_{II}}$; Cost; α	Hazard				Mixed logit			
	0.50%	3.8%	50%	Optimal	0.50%	3.8%	50%	Optimal
1	0.4868	0.0828	0.0719	0.0660*	0.2621	0.0676*	0.0748	0.0668*
10	0.4450	0.3338	0.6982	0.2672*	0.3096	0.3982	0.7263	0.2578*
20	0.4776	0.6125	1.3947	0.3591*	0.3612*	0.7652	1.4506	0.3634*
35	0.5264	1.0306	2.4396	0.4348*	0.4395*	1.3166	2.5371	0.4504*
50	0.5752	1.4486	3.4845	0.5050*	0.5177*	1.8675	3.6236	0.5324*
75	0.6565*	2.1457	5.2469	0.6333*	0.6484*	2.7864	5.4348	0.6896*
100	0.7379*	2.8427	6.9674	0.7381*	0.7785*	3.7048	7.2453	0.7677*
$\frac{Cost_I}{Cost_{II}}$; Cost; α	Rough Bayesian							
	0.50%		3.8%		50%		Optimal	
1	0.2566		0.0575*		0.0696		0.0966*	
10	0.2799		0.4886		0.7565		0.2476*	
20	0.3055*		0.7866		1.5555		0.3686*	
35	0.4866*		1.3465		2.6936		0.4279*	
50	0.5075*		1.9624		3.8796		0.5055*	
75	0.6286*		2.9690		5.7568		0.6888*	
100	0.7986*		3.9048		7.9090		0.7076*	

The optimal value is calculated through optimal cutoff point which is verified with training samples; here * denotes that at 5% significant level, the misclassification cost is statistically least in one $\frac{Cost_I}{Cost_{II}}$

Table 8.6 Random selection and test results (US companies)

	FRTDSN-HRB				FSVM			
$\frac{Cost_I}{Cost_{II}}$; Cost; α	0.50%	3.8%	50%	Optimal	0.50%	3.8%	50%	Optimal
1	0.2036	0.0750	0.0886	0.0836*	0.2054	0.0543*	0.0586	0.0548
10	0.2085	0.3569	0.6905	0.1869*	0.2496	0.4869	0.7248	0.2169*
20	0.2450*	0.7054	1.4850	0.3086*	0.2948*	0.6955	1.5055	0.3286
35	0.3048*	1.2948	2.5434	0.30438	0.3050	1.3169	2.6531	0.3679*
50	0.4872*	1.8624	3.5596	0.3855*	0.4372*	1.9619	3.8696	0.4855*
75	0.5086*	2.8672	5.3669	0.5077*	0.6686*	2.9669	5.6669	0.5577*
100	0.6888*	3.4036	7.6986	0.3675*	0.7284	3.5248	7.8186	0.6875*
	MFSVM				Bayesian			
$\frac{Cost_I}{Cost_{II}}$; Cost; α	0.50%	3.8%	50%	Optimal	0.50%	3.8%	50%	Optimal
1	0.2030	0.0434	0.0572	0.0930*	0.5272	0.2132	0.0896	0.0976*
10	0.2492	0.4069	0.7260	0.2069	0.5436	0.3128	0.4095	0.3069*
20	0.3036*	0.6955	1.5250	0.3086*	0.5420	0.4824*	0.8088	0.4848*
35	0.3148*	1.2967	2.6031	0.3643	0.5896*	0.5518*	1.4824	0.6089
50	0.4836	1.9619	3.6696	0.4855*	0.6165	0.7219	2.0960	0.5477*
75	0.5286	2.9169	5.4069	0.5077*	0.6521*	0.9602	3.1189	0.6435*
100	0.7269*	3.4848	7.7286	0.4875*	0.7070*	1.2096	4.1920	0.7069*
	Hazard				Mixed logit			
$\frac{Cost_I}{Cost_{II}}$; Cost; α	0.50%	3.8%	50%	Optimal	0.50%	3.8%	50%	Optimal
1	0.4857	0.0488	0.0710	0.0950*	0.2521	0.0655*	0.0748	0.0658*
10	0.4850	0.3036	0.6980	0.2572*	0.3090	0.3682	0.7250	0.2478*
20	0.4876	0.6025	1.4048	0.3491*	0.3610*	0.7055	1.4306	0.3133*
35	0.5064	1.0106	2.4392	0.4040*	0.4896*	1.3069	2.5071	0.4804*
50	0.5152	1.4888	3.4840	0.5040*	0.5077*	1.8175	3.6036	0.5020*
75	0.6065*	2.1057	5.2159	0.6330*	0.6081*	2.7258	5.4048	0.6196*
100	0.7079*	2.8107	6.9670	0.7380*	0.7085*	3.6948	7.2152	0.7077*
	Rough Bayesian			
$\frac{Cost_I}{Cost_{II}}$; Cost; α	0.50%	3.8%	50%	Optimal
1	0.2465	0.0477*	0.0796	0.0600*
10	0.2599	0.4069	0.7065	0.2469*
20	0.3057*	0.7850	1.6555	0.3086*
35	0.4838*	1.3067	2.6920	0.4879*
50	0.4875*	1.9620	3.8096	0.4855*
75	0.6086*	2.9689	5.7069	0.6677*
100	0.7084*	3.8948	7.8996	0.6975*

The optimal value is calculated through optimal cutoff point which is verified with training samples; here * denotes that at 5% significant level, the misclassification cost is statistically least in one $\frac{Cost_I}{Cost_{II}}$

Table 8.7 Random selection and test results (European companies)

$\frac{Cost_I}{Cost_{II}}$; Cost; α	FRTDSN-HRB				FSVM			
	0.50%	3.8%	50%	Optimal	0.50%	3.8%	50%	Optimal
1	0.2030	0.0250	0.0881	0.0800*	0.2069	0.0548*	0.0486	0.0860
10	0.2080	0.3069	0.6901	0.1769*	0.2096	0.4850	0.7043	0.2069*
20	0.2436*	0.6954	1.4848	0.3069*	0.1940*	0.6950	1.5155	0.3086
35	0.3848*	1.3050	2.5430	0.3048	0.2043	1.3067	2.6031	0.3669*
50	0.4870*	1.8620	3.5096	0.3055*	0.4072*	1.9210	3.8696	0.4850*
75	0.5069*	2.8072	5.3069	0.4877*	0.4086*	2.9660	5.6169	0.5077*
100	0.6779*	3.4838	7.6086	0.3875*	0.7086	3.5048	7.8686	0.6675*
$\frac{Cost_I}{Cost_{II}}$; Cost; α	MFSVM				Bayesian			
	0.50%	3.8%	50%	Optimal	0.50%	3.8%	50%	Optimal
1	0.2034	0.0430	0.0570	0.0800*	0.5270	0.2134	0.0892	0.0866*
10	0.2096	0.4068	0.7060	0.2169	0.5430	0.3130	0.4896	0.3060*
20	0.3030*	0.6950	1.5050	0.2986*	0.5421	0.4021*	0.8086	0.4848*
35	0.3140*	1.3060	2.6030	0.3648	0.6892*	0.5510*	1.4821	0.6080
50	0.4330	1.8919	3.6089	0.4850*	0.6160	0.7010	2.0960	0.5469*
75	0.5480	2.8969	5.3060	0.5079*	0.6921*	0.9600	3.1089	0.6036*
100	0.7069*	3.4030	7.7086	0.4886*	0.7069*	1.1996	4.1020	0.6970*
$\frac{Cost_I}{Cost_{II}}$; Cost; α	Hazard				Mixed logit			
	0.50%	3.8%	50%	Optimal	0.50%	3.8%	50%	Optimal
1	0.4850	0.0480	0.0700	0.0848*	0.2021	0.0650*	0.0740	0.0650*
10	0.4348	0.3030	0.6970	0.2570*	0.3089	0.3680	0.7050	0.2470*
20	0.4370	0.5020	1.3040	0.3489*	0.3600*	0.7050	1.4006	0.3130*
35	0.5060	1.0104	2.4892	0.4030*	0.4092*	1.3060	2.5070	0.4800*
50	0.5450	1.4380	3.4048	0.4040*	0.5070*	1.8170	3.6030	0.5010*
75	0.6050*	2.1050	5.2150	0.6030*	0.6080*	2.7250	5.4840	0.6096*
100	0.7069*	2.8106	6.9669	0.7070*	0.7080*	3.6048	7.2150	0.6977*
$\frac{Cost_I}{Cost_{II}}$; Cost; α	Rough Bayesian			
	0.50%	3.8%	50%	Optimal
1	0.2169	0.0777*	0.0592	0.0800*
10	0.2199	0.4860	0.7060	0.2169*
20	0.3050*	0.7050	1.5050	0.2986*
35	0.4010*	1.3060	2.6919	0.4070*
50	0.4070*	1.9619	3.8091	0.4850*
75	0.6080*	2.9680	5.7060	0.6070*
100	0.7888*	3.8040	7.8989	0.6970*

The optimal value is calculated through optimal cutoff point which is verified with training samples; here, * denotes that at 5% significant level, the misclassification cost is statistically least in one $\frac{Cost_I}{Cost_{II}}$

8.6   Optimal Cutoff Point: UCI Machine Learning Repository Bankruptcy Database

Here the optimal cutoff point analysis for the UCI Machine Learning bankruptcy database is presented. As discussed in the previous section, the appropriate cutoff point is computed using eq. (8.72). As discussed in Sect. 8.4, the cutoff point is estimated using the training sample. Training sample also calculates the a priori probabilities and empirical cutoff point. Prediction results are generated by the holdout sample. The cutoff points considered are 0.50%, 3.8%, and 50% for the UCI Machine Learning bankruptcy database. Paired sample t tests are performed for each pair of cutoff points. The results using various cutoff points are given in Table 8.8.

8.7   Randomly Selected Samples: Korean Construction Companies

As discussed in Sects. 8.1 and 8.2, choice of different cutoff points result in varied conclusions regarding prediction comparative power for the models considered. In this direction tests are conducted considering the distortion-free conditions considering the arbitrary cutoff point. In this process it maintains the models' true characteristics. This fact is suggested though the results highlighted in Sects. 8.3 and 8.4. This empirical cutoff point compares with other models. As in the Sects. 8.3 and 8.4, 30 random samples are utilized. Paired sample t tests generates total misclassification costs for each models' pair. The results are shown in Table 8.9 through optimal cutoff point. Considering specifications of Type I and Type II cost FRTDSN-HRB, FSVM, MFSVM, hazard, mixed logit, and rough Bayesian models perform effectively with respect to power prediction. FRTDSN-HRB has highest predictive power for the Korean construction companies' datasets. There are situations where ex post results highlight and predict the prior events through a noisy sample. This can be considered as possible drawback of the randomly selected samples.

8.8   Randomly Selected Samples: American and European Nonfinancial Companies

In similar lines with the discussion presented in Sect. 8.7, the results for the American and European nonfinancial companies' datasets are highlighted. The tests are conducted under distortion-free conditions where the true characteristics of the models are maintained. The 30 random samples are used. The paired sample t tests generate total misclassification costs. The results are presented in Tables 8.10 and 8.11 through the optimal cutoff point. FRTDSN-HRB achieves the highest predictive power for the American and European nonfinancial companies' datasets.

Table 8.8 Random selection and test results (UCI Machine Learning Repository bankruptcy database)

$\frac{Cost_I}{Cost_{II}}$; Cost; α	FRTDSN-HRB				FSVM			
	0.50%	3.8%	50%	Optimal	0.50%	3.8%	50%	Optimal
1	0.2031	0.0350	0.0881	0.0830*	0.2054	0.0548*	0.0586	0.0848
10	0.2086	0.3669	0.6905	0.1969*	0.2496	0.4069	0.7248	0.2169*
20	0.2450*	0.7054	1.4350	0.3086*	0.2948*	0.6955	1.5055	0.3286
35	0.3043*	1.2943	2.5481	0.3048	0.2948	1.3167	2.6531	0.3679*
50	0.4072*	1.8621	3.5596	0.3155*	0.4372*	1.9619	3.8196	0.4855*
75	0.5086*	2.8172	5.3669	0.5077*	0.6086*	2.9669	5.6069	0.5577*
100	0.6886*	3.4036	7.6986	0.3675*	0.7284	3.5248	7.8186	0.6875*
$\frac{Cost_I}{Cost_{II}}$; Cost; α	MFSVM				Bayesian			
	0.50%	3.8%	50%	Optimal	0.50%	3.8%	50%	Optimal
1	0.2030	0.0434	0.0572	0.0630*	0.5272	0.2132	0.0896	0.0976*
10	0.2492	0.4869	0.7260	0.2069	0.5436	0.3128	0.4095	0.2969*
20	0.2935*	0.6955	1.5250	0.3086*	0.5420	0.4024*	0.8087	0.4348*
35	0.3143*	1.3068	2.6031	0.3648	0.5892*	0.5518*	1.4324	0.6089
50	0.4336	1.9219	3.6096	0.4855*	0.6165	0.7210	2.0960	0.5470*
75	0.5286	2.9169	5.4069	0.5077*	0.6521*	0.9602	3.1189	0.6435*
100	0.7269*	3.4048	7.7286	0.4875*	0.7070*	1.2092	4.1920	0.7069*
$\frac{Cost_I}{Cost_{II}}$; Cost; α	Hazard				Mixed logit			
	0.50%	3.8%	50%	Optimal	0.50%	3.8%	50%	Optimal
1	0.4069	0.0488	0.0719	0.0950*	0.2524	0.0655*	0.0748	0.0658*
10	0.4350	0.3036	0.6980	0.2572*	0.2990	0.3682	0.7250	0.2478*
20	0.4376	0.6025	1.3940	0.3491*	0.3610*	0.7055	1.4806	0.3133*
35	0.5064	1.0106	2.4392	0.4048*	0.4396*	1.3066	2.5071	0.4804*
50	0.5152	1.4388	3.4840	0.5040*	0.5077*	1.8175	3.6036	0.5020*
75	0.6065*	2.1057	5.2169	0.6930*	0.6081*	2.7258	5.4048	0.6196*
100	0.7079*	2.8107	6.9670	0.7380*	0.7085*	3.6940	7.2153	0.7077*
$\frac{Cost_I}{Cost_{II}}$; Cost; α	Rough Bayesian							
	0.50%		3.8%		50%		Optimal	
1	0.2466		0.0475*		0.0596		0.0900*	
10	0.2599		0.4069		0.7065		0.2469*	
20	0.2957*		0.7850		1.5055		0.3086*	
35	0.4830*		1.3067		2.6920		0.4879*	
50	0.4875*		1.9620		3.8096		0.4855*	
75	0.6086*		2.9689		5.7069		0.6977*	
100	0.7084*		3.8948		7.8990		0.6975*	

The optimal value is calculated through optimal cutoff point which is verified with training samples; here, * denotes that at 5% significant level the misclassification cost is statistically least in one $\frac{Cost_I}{Cost_{II}}$

Table 8.9 The costs of misclassification (Korean companies)

$\frac{Cost_I}{Cost_{II}}$	FRTDSN-HRB	FSVM	MFSVM	Bayesian	Hazard	Mixed logit	Rough Bayesian
1	0.0648*	0.0659*	0.0650*	0.0770	0.0650*	0.0661*	0.0660*
10	0.2019*	0.2069*	0.2068*	0.2970	0.2170*	0.2472*	0.2169*
20	0.3040*	0.3080*	0.3070*	0.4340	0.3491*	0.3630*	0.3086*
35	0.4048*	0.4070*	0.4050*	0.6280	0.4336*	0.4888*	0.4079*
50	0.5020*	0.5048*	0.5030*	0.5770	0.5043*	0.5319*	0.5050*
75	0.6750*	0.6769*	0.6760*	0.6530*	0.6836*	0.6896*	0.6879*
100	0.7040*	0.7060*	0.7050*	0.7069*	0.7380*	0.7670*	0.7070*

Here * indicates the least cost at 5% significance level

Table 8.10 The costs of misclassification (US companies)

$\frac{Cost_I}{Cost_{II}}$	FRTDSN-HRB	FSVM	MFSVM	Bayesian	Hazard	Mixed logit	Rough Bayesian
1	0.0648*	0.0659*	0.0650*	0.0779	0.0650*	0.0666*	0.0660*
10	0.2019*	0.2069*	0.2060*	0.2970	0.2170*	0.2472*	0.2169*
20	0.3040*	0.3080*	0.3070*	0.4348	0.3491*	0.3630*	0.3086*
35	0.4040*	0.4070*	0.4050*	0.6286	0.4338*	0.4800*	0.4079*
50	0.5020*	0.5040*	0.5030*	0.5779	0.5043*	0.5319*	0.5060*
75	0.6750*	0.6769*	0.6760*	0.6536*	0.6936*	0.6896*	0.6770*
100	0.7040*	0.7060*	0.7075*	0.7069*	0.7386*	0.7670*	0.7979*

Here * indicates the least cost at 5% significance level

Table 8.11 The costs of misclassification (European companies)

$\frac{Cost_I}{Cost_{II}}$	FRTDSN-HRB	FSVM	MFSVM	Bayesian	Hazard	Mixed logit	Rough Bayesian
1	0.0648*	0.0650*	0.0640*	0.0769	0.0640*	0.0660*	0.0650*
10	0.2010*	0.2060*	0.2050*	0.2968	0.2165*	0.2470*	0.2161*
20	0.3036*	0.3070*	0.3060*	0.4330	0.3481*	0.3620*	0.3879*
35	0.4030*	0.4065*	0.4048*	0.6270	0.4325*	0.4800*	0.4079*
50	0.5010*	0.5035*	0.5020*	0.5760	0.5033*	0.5310*	0.5040*
75	0.6848*	0.6760*	0.6750*	0.6520*	0.6320*	0.6880*	0.6760*
100	0.7938*	0.7055*	0.7040*	0.7060*	0.7379*	0.7969*	0.7060*

Here * indicates the least cost at 5% significance level

Table 8.12 The costs of misclassification (UCI Machine Learning Repository bankruptcy database)

$\frac{Cost_I}{Cost_{II}}$	FRTDSN-HRB	FSVM	MFSVM	Bayesian	Hazard	Mixed logit	Rough Bayesian
1	0.0640*	0.0669*	0.0650*	0.0770	0.0650*	0.0661*	0.0669*
10	0.2019*	0.2069*	0.2060*	0.2970	0.2170*	0.2472*	0.2169*
20	0.3048*	0.3080*	0.3070*	0.4340	0.3496*	0.3630*	0.3086*
35	0.4048*	0.4070*	0.4050*	0.6280	0.4335*	0.4500*	0.4079*
50	0.5020*	0.5040*	0.5030*	0.5770	0.5043*	0.5319*	0.5050*
75	0.6950*	0.6769*	0.6760*	0.6530*	0.6550*	0.6896*	0.6979*
100	0.7948*	0.7090*	0.7050*	0.7069*	0.7380*	0.7670*	0.7070*

Here * indicates the least cost at 5% significance level

8.9   Randomly Selected Samples: UCI Machine Learning Repository Bankruptcy Database

In similar lines with the discussion presented in Sect. 8.8, the results for the UCI Machine Learning bankruptcy database are highlighted. As in the previous section, the tests are conducted under distortion-free conditions. The 30 random samples are utilized. The paired sample t tests generate total misclassification costs. The results are presented in Table 8.12 through the optimal cutoff point. FRTDSN-HRB achieves the highest predictive power for the UCI Machine Learning bankruptcy database.

8.10   Samples in Full and Sub-business Cycles: Korean Construction Companies

In this section the samples in full and sub-business cycle analysis for the Korean construction companies are highlighted. The analysis conducted across business cycles as random selection gives distorted results with noisy samples. The sample consists of four business cycles. The adjacent business cycles are used for the comparative analysis. The preceding cycle helps to calculate the priors, estimates, and optimal cutoff points. The subsequent cycles help to calculate the misclassification cost. The initial two cycles are combined because of the short nature of the first business cycle and small sample size. Tables 8.13 and 8.14 highlight the results on full and sub-business cycles. Tables 8.13 and 8.14 denote that optimal cutoff point decreases when the Type I error cost goes up. The decrease happens when Type II error shoots up. From Tables 8.13 and 8.14, $\frac{Cost_I}{Cost_{II}}$ increases when cutoff point goes down considerably. These results contradict the randomly selected samples results considering the total cost. In general FRTDSN-HRB outperforms other models. These results are in line for tests considering the sub-cycles. Figures 8.1, 8.2, 8.3, 8.4, 8.5, 8.6, 8.7, 8.8, 8.9, 8.10, 8.11, 8.12, 8.13, and 8.14 use

Table 8.13 The results estimated across business cycles (Korean companies)

	FRTDSN-HRB		FSVM		MFSVM	
Panel A						
$\frac{Cost_I}{Cost_{II}}$	1st and 2nd cycle → 3rd cycle					
	Best	Normal	Best	Normal	Best	Normal
5	5.4821	0.1430	0.0291	**0.0896**	0.0750	0.1170
15	0.0119	0.3789	0.0001	0.3686	0.0092	0.2796
25	0.0119	0.4030	0.0001	0.4096	0.0040	0.3550
40	0.0119	0.4300	0.0001	0.4704	0.0030	0.4886
60	0.0119	0.4770	0.0001	0.5320	0.0030	0.5196
80	0.0119	0.5380	0.0001	0.7613	0.0030	0.6219
100	9.67e-4	0.7230	0.0001	0.8630	0.0036	0.7230
Panel B						
$\frac{Cost_I}{Cost_{II}}$	3rd cycle → 4th cycle					
	Best	Normal	Best	Normal	Best	Normal
5	1.5004	0.0710	0.2740	0.0592	0.4020	0.0592
15	0.1986	0.2792	0.0120	0.2038	0.0800	0.3540
25	0.0280	0.5088	0.0080	0.2748	0.0800	0.5989
40	0.0230	0.5570	0.0070	0.3760	0.0616	0.5710
60	0.0230	0.5980	0.0050	0.4680	0.0290	0.5419
80	0.0230	0.6660	0.0050	0.5810	0.0290	0.6092
100	0.0230	0.7348	0.0050	0.6948	0.0290	0.6777

	Bayesian		Hazard		Mixed logit		Rough Bayesian	
Panel A								
$\frac{Cost_I}{Cost_{II}}$	1st and 2nd cycle → 3rd cycle							
	Best	Normal	Best	Normal	Best	Normal	Best	Normal
5	5.4821	0.1433	0.0293	0.0896	0.0751	0.1172	0.0776	0.1279
15	0.0119	0.3792	0.0002	0.3687	0.0099	0.2796	0.0100	0.2595
25	0.0119	0.4036	0.0002	0.4096	0.0041	0.3553	0.0083	0.3548
40	0.0119	0.4801	0.0002	0.4709	0.0038	0.4583	0.0072	0.4801
60	0.0119	0.4771	0.0002	0.5321	0.0038	0.5193	0.0079	0.5053
80	0.0119	0.5381	0.0001	0.7619	0.0038	0.6219	0.0069	0.6072
100	9.6e-5	0.7231	0.0001	0.8638	0.0038	0.7233	0.0068	0.7353
Panel B								
$\frac{Cost_I}{Cost_{II}}$	3rd cycle → 4th cycle							
	Best	Normal	Best	Normal	Best	Normal	Best	Normal
5	1.5009	0.0719	0.2741	0.0595	0.4124	0.0596	0.4038	0.0598
15	0.1889	0.2796	0.0199	0.2031	0.0805	0.3540	0.1665	0.2578
25	0.0284	0.5080	0.0087	0.2747	0.0805	0.5089	0.0554	0.4595
40	0.0234	0.5578	0.0076	0.3760	0.0616	0.5713	0.0198	0.3998
60	0.0234	0.5986	0.0059	0.4882	0.0289	0.5413	0.0238	0.5274
80	0.0234	0.6665	0.0059	0.5811	0.0289	0.6093	0.0238	0.6284
100	0.0234	0.7345	0.0059	0.6941	0.0289	0.6774	0.0238	0.7236

Table 8.14 The results estimated across mid-cycles (Korean companies)

	FRTDSN-HRB		FSVM		MFSVM	
Panel A						
$\frac{Cost_I}{Cost_{II}}$	**6th mid-cycle → 7th mid-cycle**					
	Best	**Normal**	**Best**	**Normal**	**Best**	**Normal**
5	0.3670	0.1734	0.3673	0.1936	0.3671	0.1735
15	0.1050	0.7586	0.1053	0.7588	0.1051	0.7587
25	0.0730	0.3370	0.0733	0.3372	0.0731	0.3371
40	0.0736	0.5250	0.0733	0.5253	0.0731	0.5251
60	0.0286	0.8286	0.0281	0.8281	0.0280	0.8280
80	0.0286	1.2820	0.0281	1.2121	0.0280	1.2120
100	0.0286	1.5570	0.0281	1.5572	0.0280	1.5571
Panel B						
$\frac{Cost_I}{Cost_{II}}$	**7th mid-cycle → 8th cycle**					
	Best	**Normal**	**Best**	**Normal**	**Best**	**Normal**
5	0.0336	0.1276	0.0337	0.1278	0.0338	0.1277
15	0.0001	0.4036	0.0001	0.4040	0.0001	0.4038
25	0.0001	0.2536	0.0001	0.2538	0.0001	0.2640
40	0.0001	0.3674	0.0001	0.3675	0.0001	0.3676
60	0.0001	0.4896	0.0001	0.4898	0.0001	0.4897
80	0.0001	0.7270	0.0001	0.7271	0.0001	0.7271
100	0.0001	0.8082	0.0001	0.8085	0.0001	0.8083

	Bayesian		Hazard		Mixed logit		Rough Bayesian	
Panel A								
$\frac{Cost_I}{Cost_{II}}$	**6th mid-cycle → 7th mid-cycle**							
	Best	**Normal**	**Best**	**Normal**	**Best**	**Normal**	**Best**	**Normal**
5	0.4838	0.2463	0.2637	0.2676	0.3706	0.1739	0.3675	0.1748
15	0.1965	1.1739	0.0154	0.5352	0.1137	0.8985	0.1055	0.7589
25	0.0829	1.7971	0.0086	0.6901	0.0629	0.3478	0.0735	0.3376
40	0.0193	0.5942	0.0073	1.1267	0.0629	0.5652	0.0735	0.5255
60	0.0193	0.8119	0.0060	1.5492	0.0286	0.8695	0.0282	0.8282
80	0.0193	1.1939	0.0060	2.2535	0.0286	1.2318	0.0282	1.2122
100	0.0193	1.5362	0.0060	2.9577	0.0286	1.5948	0.0282	1.5575
Panel B								
$\frac{Cost_I}{Cost_{II}}$	**7th mid-cycle → 8th cycle**							
	Best	**Normal**	**Best**	**Normal**	**Best**	**Normal**	**Best**	**Normal**
5	0.7672	0.1158	0.0003	0.1003	0.0336	0.2406	0.0348	0.1979
15	0.0386	0.6771	0.0002	0.2067	0.0002	0.3921	0.0001	0.4040
25	0.0386	0.6868	0.0002	0.2743	0.0002	0.4405	0.0001	0.2848
40	0.0386	0.7013	0.0002	0.3757	0.0002	0.5130	0.0001	0.3676
60	0.0386	0.7158	0.0002	0.4771	0.0002	0.5855	0.0001	0.4899
80	0.0386	0.7400	0.0002	0.6462	0.0002	0.7061	0.0001	0.7271
100	0.0386	0.7648	0.0002	0.8653	0.0002	0.8270	0.0001	0.8086

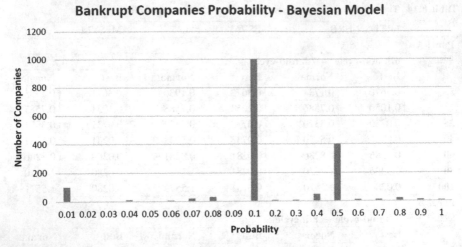

Fig. 8.1 Bankrupt companies' probability, Bayesian model (Korean companies)

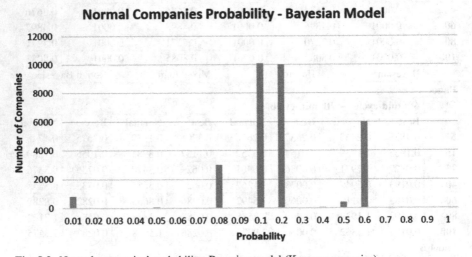

Fig. 8.2 Normal companies' probability, Bayesian model (Korean companies)

the randomly selected sample that provides the probability of estimation with respect to the companies considering the normal and bankrupt picture. Here horizontal axis represents probability and vertical axis represents the number of companies.

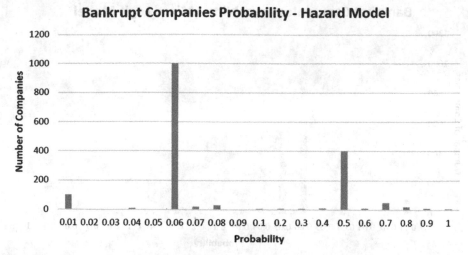

Fig. 8.3 Bankrupt companies' probability, hazard model (Korean companies)

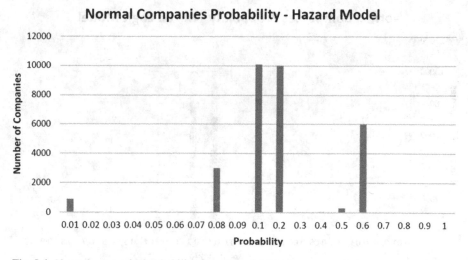

Fig. 8.4 Normal companies probability, hazard model (Korean companies)

8.11 Samples in Full and Sub-business Cycles: American and European Nonfinancial Companies

In this section the samples in full and sub-business cycle analysis for the American and European nonfinancial companies' datasets are highlighted. The random selection produces results distorted with the noisy samples. As a result of this, the analysis is conducted across the four business cycles with the adjacent business cycles for the comparative analysis. The preceding cycle helps to calculate the

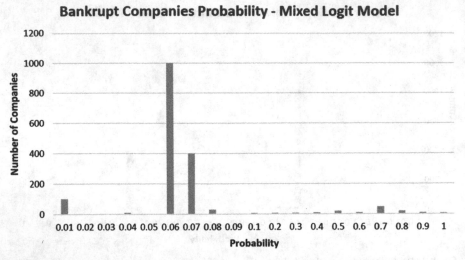

Fig. 8.5 Bankrupt companies' probability, mixed logit model (Korean companies)

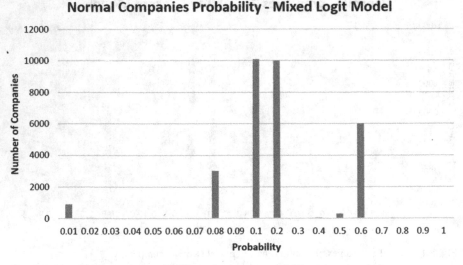

Fig. 8.6 Normal companies' probability, mixed logit model (Korean companies)

priors, estimates, and optimal cutoff points. The subsequent cycles help to calculate the misclassification cost. The initial two cycles are combined because of the short nature of the first business cycle and small sample size. Tables 8.15, 8.16, 8.17, and 8.18 highlight the results on full and sub-business cycles. Tables 8.15, 8.16, 8.17, and 8.18 denote that the Type I error cost goes up as the optimal cutoff point goes down. From Tables 8.15, 8.16, 8.17, and 8.18, the conclusion is that as $\frac{Cost_I}{Cost_{II}}$ becomes greater, cutoff point goes down considerably. In general FRTDSN-HRB outperforms other models. These results are in line for tests on the sub-cycles.

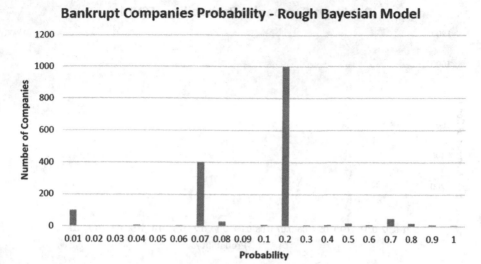

Fig. 8.7 Bankrupt companies' probability, rough Bayesian model (Korean companies)

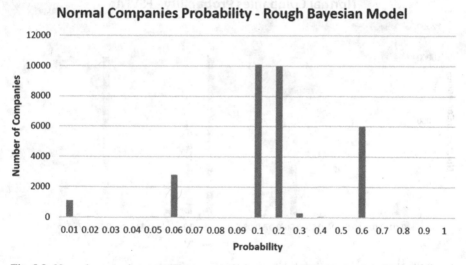

Fig. 8.8 Normal companies probability, rough Bayesian model (Korean companies)

Figures 8.15, 8.16, 8.17, 8.18, 8.19, 8.20, 8.21, 8.22, 8.23, 8.24, 8.25, 8.26, 8.27, 8.28, 8.29, 8.30, 8.31, 8.32, 8.33, 8.34, 8.35, 8.36, 8.37, 8.38, 8.39, 8.40, 8.41, and 8.42 use the randomly selected sample that gives the probability estimation for companies having normal and bankrupt picture.

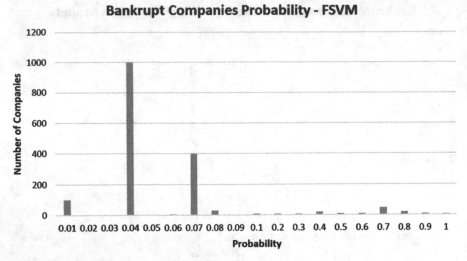

Fig. 8.9 Bankrupt companies' probability, FSVM (Korean companies)

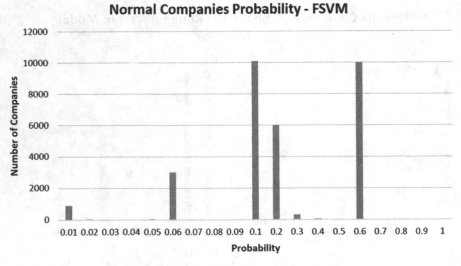

Fig. 8.10 Normal companies' probability, FSVM (Korean companies)

8.12   Samples in Full and Sub-business Cycles: UCI Machine Learning Repository Bankruptcy Database

In this section the samples in full and sub-business cycle analysis for the UCI Machine Learning bankruptcy database are highlighted. The random selection yields results distorted with the noisy samples. Hence the analysis is conducted across the four business cycles with the adjacent business cycles for the

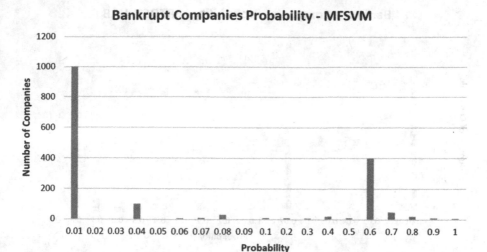

Fig. 8.11 Bankrupt companies' probability, MFSVM (Korean companies)

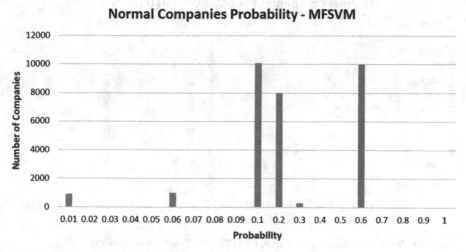

Fig. 8.12 Normal companies' probability, MFSVM (Korean companies)

comparative analysis. The preceding cycle calculates the priors, estimates, and optimal cutoff points. As discussed in previous section, the subsequent cycles are considered to calculate the misclassification cost. The initial two cycles are combined because of the short nature of the first business cycle and small sample size. Tables 8.19 and 8.20 highlight the results on full and sub-business cycles. Tables 8.19 and 8.20 show that optimal cutoff point decreases as the Type I error cost goes up. From Tables 8.19 and 8.20, when $\frac{Cost_I}{Cost_{II}}$ increases, cutoff point goes

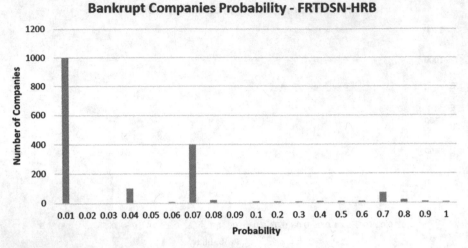

Fig. 8.13 Bankrupt companies probability, FRTDSN-HRB (Korean companies)

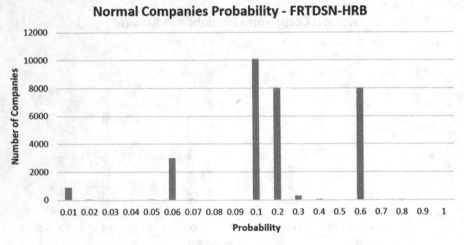

Fig. 8.14 Normal companies' probability, FRTDSN-HRB (Korean companies)

down considerably. As in other datasets, FRTDSN-HRB achieves superior performance. These results are in line with tests on the sub-cycles. Figures 8.43, 8.44, 8.45, 8.46, 8.47, 8.48, 8.49, 8.50, 8.51, 8.52, 8.53, 8.54, 8.55, and 8.56 use the randomly selected sample that gives probability of estimation with respect to the companies considering normal and bankrupt and normal picture.

Table 8.15 The results estimated across business cycles (US companies)

	FRTDSN-HRB		FSVM		MFSVM	
Panel A						
$\frac{Cost_L}{Cost_{II}}$	**1st and 2nd cycle → 3rd cycle**					
	Best	**Normal**	**Best**	**Normal**	**Best**	**Normal**
5	5.4520	0.1429	0.0291	**0.0891**	0.0749	0.1169
15	0.0120	0.3788	0.0001	0.3685	0.0091	0.2795
25	0.0120	0.4029	0.0001	0.4896	0.0038	0.3650
40	0.0120	0.4300	0.0001	0.4703	0.0030	0.4879
60	0.0120	0.4769	0.0001	0.5319	0.0030	0.5191
80	0.0120	0.5379	0.0001	0.7611	0.0030	0.6209
100	9.67e-3	0.7130	0.0001	0.8629	0.0030	0.7130
Panel B						
$\frac{Cost_L}{Cost_{II}}$	**3rd cycle → 4th cycle**					
	Best	**Normal**	**Best**	**Normal**	**Best**	**Normal**
5	1.5003	0.0709	0.2738	0.0591	0.4019	0.0591
15	0.1979	0.2791	0.0119	0.2029	0.0800	0.3638
25	0.0279	0.5079	0.0079	0.2738	0.0800	0.4987
40	0.0230	0.5569	0.0069	0.3760	0.0613	0.5709
60	0.0230	0.5979	0.0050	0.4679	0.0289	0.5409
80	0.0230	0.6660	0.0050	0.5809	0.0289	0.6091
100	0.0230	0.7338	0.0050	0.6938	0.0289	0.6869

	Bayesian		Hazard		Mixed logit		Rough Bayesian	
Panel A								
$\frac{Cost_L}{Cost_{II}}$	**1st and 2nd cycle → 3rd cycle**							
	Best	**Normal**	**Best**	**Normal**	**Best**	**Normal**	**Best**	**Normal**
5	5.4820	0.1432	0.0292	0.0895	0.0750	0.1171	0.0774	0.1970
15	0.0119	0.3791	0.0002	0.3686	0.0098	0.2795	0.0099	0.2596
25	0.0119	0.4035	0.0002	0.4095	0.0048	0.3552	0.0081	0.3548
40	0.0119	0.4400	0.0002	0.4708	0.0036	0.4582	0.0071	0.4800
60	0.0119	0.4770	0.0002	0.5320	0.0036	0.5192	0.0070	0.5054
80	0.0119	0.5380	0.0001	0.7613	0.0036	0.6211	0.0068	0.6072
100	9.67e-4	0.7230	0.0001	0.8633	0.0036	0.7231	0.0067	0.7354
Panel B								
$\frac{Cost_L}{Cost_{II}}$	**3rd cycle → 4th cycle**							
	Best	**Normal**	**Best**	**Normal**	**Best**	**Normal**	**Best**	**Normal**
5	1.5008	0.0719	0.2748	0.0996	0.4121	0.0595	0.4029	0.0597
15	0.1988	0.2795	0.0129	0.2030	0.0803	0.3538	0.1662	0.2577
25	0.0284	0.5079	0.0086	0.2743	0.0803	0.4987	0.0552	0.4594
40	0.0234	0.5577	0.0074	0.3760	0.0613	0.5719	0.0197	0.3999
60	0.0234	0.5985	0.0068	0.4881	0.0287	0.5419	0.0237	0.5272
80	0.0234	0.6664	0.0068	0.5810	0.0287	0.6092	0.0237	0.6281
100	0.0234	0.7343	0.0068	0.6940	0.0287	0.6772	0.0237	0.7230

Table 8.16 The results estimated across mid-cycles (US companies)

	FRTDSN-HRB		FSVM		MFSVM	
Panel A						
$\frac{\text{Cost}_I}{\text{Cost}_{II}}$	**6th mid-cycle → 7th mid-cycle**					
	Best	Normal	Best	Normal	Best	Normal
5	0.3669	0.1733	0.3672	0.1735	0.3670	0.1734
15	0.1050	0.7585	0.1052	0.7587	0.1050	0.7586
25	0.0730	0.3369	0.0734	0.3371	0.0730	0.3470
40	0.0730	0.5249	0.0734	0.5454	0.0730	0.5450
60	0.0279	0.8279	0.0280	0.8286	0.0279	0.8279
80	0.0279	1.2119	0.0280	1.2120	0.0279	1.2119
100	0.0279	1.5569	0.0280	1.5571	0.0279	1.5570
Panel B						
$\frac{\text{Cost}_I}{\text{Cost}_{II}}$	**7th mid-cycle → 8th cycle**					
	Best	Normal	Best	Normal	Best	Normal
5	0.0335	0.1275	0.0336	0.1277	0.0337	0.1276
15	0.0001	0.4035	0.0001	0.4038	0.0001	0.4038
25	0.0001	0.2536	0.0001	0.2537	0.0001	0.2638
40	0.0001	0.3673	0.0001	0.3674	0.0001	0.3675
60	0.0001	0.4895	0.0001	0.4897	0.0001	0.4896
80	0.0001	0.7269	0.0001	0.7270	0.0001	0.7270
100	0.0001	0.8081	0.0001	0.8083	0.0001	0.8081

	Bayesian		Hazard		Mixed logit		Rough Bayesian	
Panel A								
$\frac{\text{Cost}_I}{\text{Cost}_{II}}$	**6th mid-cycle → 7th mid-cycle**							
	Best	Normal	Best	Normal	Best	Normal	Best	Normal
5	0.4034	0.2466	0.2636	0.2675	0.3705	0.1738	0.3677	0.1738
15	0.1964	1.1738	0.0153	0.5351	0.1136	0.8984	0.1054	0.7588
25	0.0829	1.7970	0.0083	0.6900	0.0629	0.3477	0.0734	0.3375
40	0.0192	0.5941	0.0072	1.1266	0.0629	0.5651	0.0734	0.5254
60	0.0192	0.8119	0.0068	1.5491	0.0284	0.8696	0.0286	0.8286
80	0.0192	1.1938	0.0068	2.2534	0.0284	1.2419	0.0286	1.2136
100	0.0192	1.5361	0.0068	2.9676	0.0284	1.6948	0.0286	1.5574
Panel B								
$\frac{\text{Cost}_I}{\text{Cost}_{II}}$	**7th mid-cycle → 8th cycle**							
	Best	Normal	Best	Normal	Best	Normal	Best	Normal
5	0.7679	0.1157	0.0002	0.1002	0.0335	0.2404	0.0338	0.1278
15	0.0379	0.6770	0.0001	0.2066	0.0001	0.3920	0.0001	0.4838
25	0.0379	0.6867	0.0001	0.2741	0.0001	0.4401	0.0001	0.2738
40	0.0379	0.7011	0.0001	0.3755	0.0001	0.5 129	0.0001	0.3674
60	0.0379	0.7157	0.0001	0.4870	0.0001	0.5853	0.0001	0.4898
80	0.0379	0.7400	0.0001	0.6464	0.0001	0.7060	0.0001	0.7276
100	0.0379	0.7638	0.0001	0.8651	0.0001	0.8269	0.0001	0.8086

Table 8.17 The results estimated across business cycles (European companies)

	FRTDSN-HRB		FSVM		MFSVM	
Panel A						
$\frac{Cost_I}{Cost_{II}}$	1st and 2nd cycle → 3rd cycle					
	Best	**Normal**	**Best**	**Normal**	**Best**	**Normal**
5	5.4519	0.1427	0.0289	0.0889	0.0747	0.1168
15	0.0111	0.3787	0.0001	0.3683	0.0089	0.2792
25	0.0111	0.4027	0.0001	0.4092	0.0040	0.3547
40	0.0111	0.4300	0.0001	0.4701	0.0028	0.4578
60	0.0111	0.4768	0.0001	0.5318	0.0028	0.5189
80	0.0111	0.5378	0.0001	0.7611	0.0028	0.6208
100	9.67e-2	0.7227	0.0001	0.8627	0.0028	0.7227
Panel B						
$\frac{Cost_I}{Cost_{II}}$	3rd cycle → 4th cycle					
	Best	**Normal**	**Best**	**Normal**	**Best**	**Normal**
5	1.5003	0.0708	0.2738	0.0589	0.4018	0.0589
15	0.1878	0.2789	0.0118	0.2028	0.0800	0.3538
25	0.0278	0.5078	0.0078	0.2738	0.0800	0.4986
40	0.0227	0.5568	0.0068	0.3758	0.0614	0.5708
60	0.0227	0.5978	0.0047	0.4678	0.0288	0.5408
80	0.0227	0.6658	0.0047	0.5808	0.0288	0.6089
100	0.0227	0.7338	0.0047	0.6938	0.0288	0.6768

	Bayesian		Hazard		Mixed logit		Rough Bayesian	
Panel A								
$\frac{Cost_I}{Cost_{II}}$	1st and 2nd cycle → 3rd cycle							
	Best	**Normal**	**Best**	**Normal**	**Best**	**Normal**	**Best**	**Normal**
5	5.4520	0.1432	0.0292	0.0896	0.0750	0.1171	0.0777	0.1270
15	0.0112	0.3791	0.0002	0.3686	0.0098	0.2795	0.0100	0.2594
25	0.0112	0.4035	0.0002	0.4095	0.0040	0.3552	0.0082	0.3547
40	0.0112	0.4400	0.0002	0.4708	0.0030	0.4582	0.0071	0.4400
60	0.0112	0.4770	0.0002	0.5320	0.0030	0.5192	0.0070	0.5051
80	0.0112	0.5380	0.0001	0.7613	0.0030	0.6211	0.0068	0.6071
100	9.6e-2	0.7230	0.0001	0.8633	0.0030	0.7232	0.0067	0.7351
Panel B								
$\frac{Cost_I}{Cost_{II}}$	3rd cycle → 4th cycle							
	Best	**Normal**	**Best**	**Normal**	**Best**	**Normal**	**Best**	**Normal**
5	1.5008	0.0711	0.2740	0.0594	0.4121	0.0595	0.4028	0.0600
15	0.1988	0.2795	0.0127	0.2030	0.0803	0.3538	0.1664	0.2577
25	0.0283	0.5079	0.0086	0.2743	0.0803	0.4988	0.0553	0.4594
40	0.0233	0.5577	0.0074	0.3758	0.0613	0.5711	0.0199	0.4000
60	0.0233	0.5985	0.0058	0.4680	0.0288	0.5411	0.0236	0.5475
80	0.0233	0.6664	0.0058	0.5810	0.0288	0.6092	0.0236	0.6282
100	0.0233	0.7343	0.0058	0.6940	0.0288	0.6771	0.0236	0.7221

Table 8.18 The results estimated across mid-cycles (European companies)

	FRTDSN-HRB		FSVM		MFSVM	
Panel A						
$\frac{Cost_I}{Cost_{II}}$	**6th mid-cycle → 7th mid-cycle**					
	Best	**Normal**	**Best**	**Normal**	**Best**	**Normal**
5	0.3668	0.1731	0.3671	0.1734	0.3669	0.1933
15	0.1048	0.7585	0.1051	0.7586	0.1050	0.7585
25	0.0728	0.3368	0.0731	0.3370	0.0730	0.3369
40	0.0728	0.5248	0.0731	0.5453	0.0730	0.5249
60	0.0278	0.8278	0.0279	0.8279	0.0278	0.8279
80	0.0278	1.2119	0.0279	1.2119	0.0278	1.2119
100	0.0278	1.5568	0.0279	1.5570	0.0278	1.5569
Panel B						
$\frac{Cost_I}{Cost_{II}}$	**7th mid-cycle → 8th cycle**					
	Best	**Normal**	**Best**	**Normal**	**Best**	**Normal**
5	0.0334	0.1274	0.0335	0.1276	0.0336	0.1975
15	0.0001	0.4034	0.0001	0.4038	0.0001	0.4836
25	0.0001	0.2534	0.0001	0.2536	0.0001	0.2638
40	0.0001	0.3671	0.0001	0.3673	0.0001	0.3674
60	0.0001	0.4894	0.0001	0.4896	0.0001	0.4895
80	0.0001	0.7270	0.0001	0.7269	0.0001	0.7269
100	0.0001	0.8080	0.0001	0.8083	0.0001	0.8086

	Bayesian		Hazard		Mixed logit		Rough Bayesian	
Panel A								
$\frac{Cost_I}{Cost_{II}}$	**6th mid-cycle → 7th mid-cycle**							
	Best	**Normal**	**Best**	**Normal**	**Best**	**Normal**	**Best**	**Normal**
5	0.4034	0.2462	0.2636	0.2675	0.3705	0.1738	0.3674	0.2038
15	0.1964	1.1738	0.0153	0.5351	0.1136	0.8984	0.1054	0.7588
25	0.0828	1.7970	0.0084	0.6900	0.0628	0.3477	0.0734	0.3379
40	0.0193	0.5941	0.0072	1.1266	0.0628	0.5651	0.0734	0.5254
60	0.0193	0.8114	0.0069	1.5491	0.0284	0.8694	0.0286	0.8286
80	0.0193	1.1738	0.0069	2.2534	0.0284	1.2317	0.0286	1.2136
100	0.0193	1.5364	0.0069	2.9576	0.0284	1.5948	0.0286	1.5577
Panel B								
$\frac{Cost_I}{Cost_{II}}$	**7th mid-cycle → 8th cycle**							
	Best	**Normal**	**Best**	**Normal**	**Best**	**Normal**	**Best**	**Normal**
5	0.7671	0.1157	0.0002	0.1002	0.0335	0.2404	0.0338	0.1278
15	0.0379	0.6770	0.0001	0.2066	0.0001	0.3920	0.0001	0.4038
25	0.0379	0.6867	0.0001	0.2741	0.0001	0.4401	0.0001	0.2738
40	0.0379	0.7011	0.0001	0.3755	0.0001	0.5129	0.0001	0.3674
60	0.0379	0.7157	0.0001	0.4770	0.0001	0.5854	0.0001	0.4898
80	0.0379	0.7400	0.0001	0.6461	0.0001	0.7060	0.0001	0.7270
100	0.0379	0.7638	0.0001	0.8151	0.0001	0.8268	0.0001	0.8085

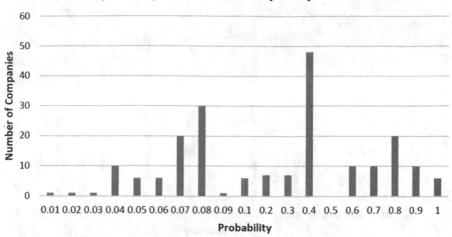

Fig. 8.15 Bankrupt companies' probability, Bayesian model (US companies)

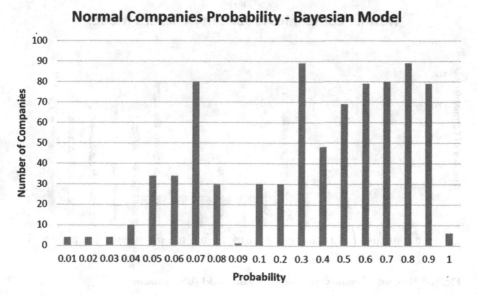

Fig. 8.16 Normal companies' probability, Bayesian model (US companies)

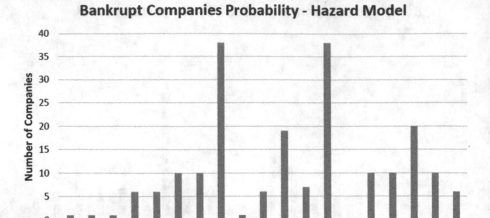

Fig. 8.17 Bankrupt companies probability, hazard model (US companies)

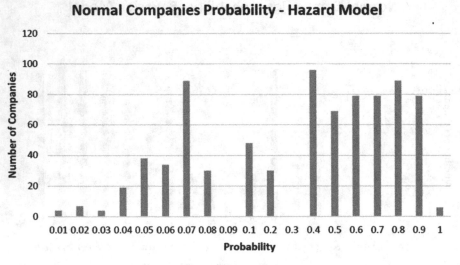

Fig. 8.18 Normal companies' probability, hazard model (US companies)

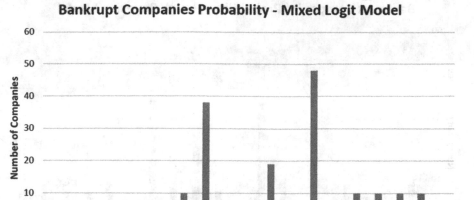

Fig. 8.19 Bankrupt companies probability, mixed logit model (US companies)

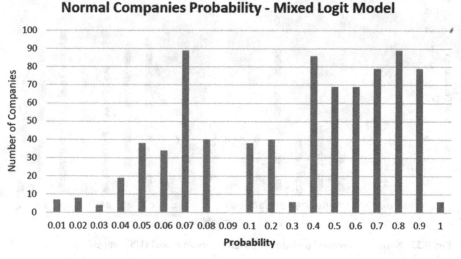

Fig. 8.20 Normal companies probability, mixed logit model (US companies)

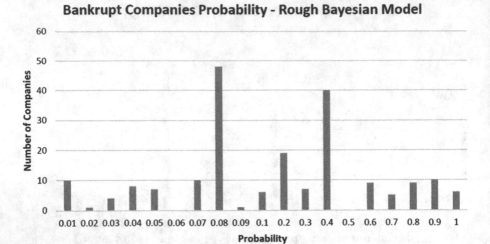

Fig. 8.21 Bankrupt companies' probability, rough Bayesian model (US companies)

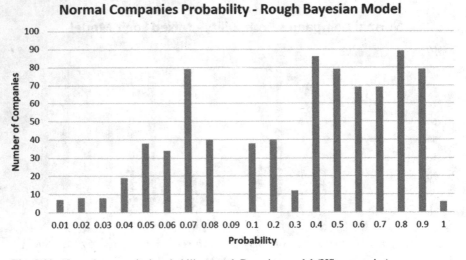

Fig. 8.22 Normal companies' probability, rough Bayesian model (US companies)

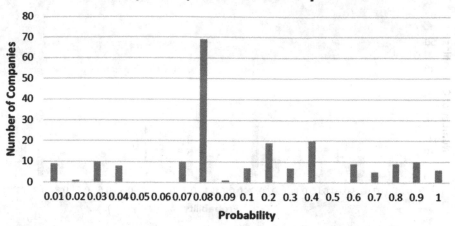

Fig. 8.23   Bankrupt companies' probability, FSVM (US companies)

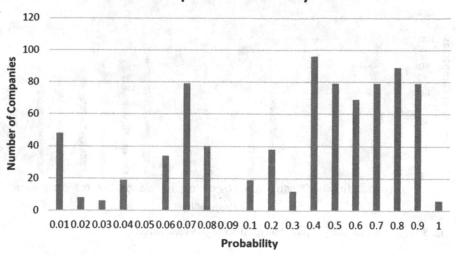

Fig. 8.24   Normal companies' probability, FSVM (US companies)

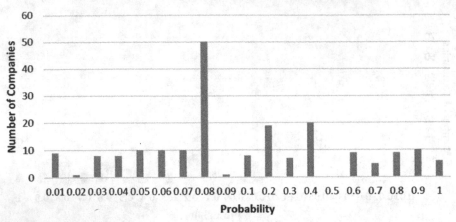

Fig. 8.25 Bankrupt companies' probability, MFSVM (US companies)

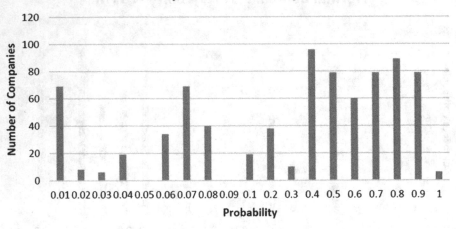

Fig. 8.26 Normal companies' probability, MFSVM (US companies)

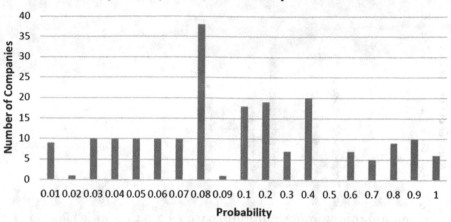

Fig. 8.27 Bankrupt companies' probability, FRTDSN-HRB (US companies)

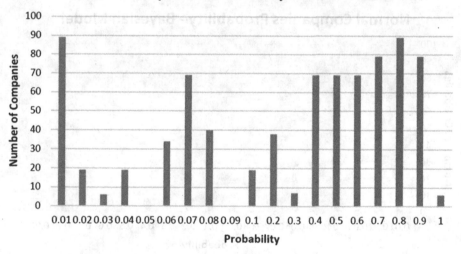

Fig. 8.28 Normal companies' probability, FRTDSN-HRB (US companies)

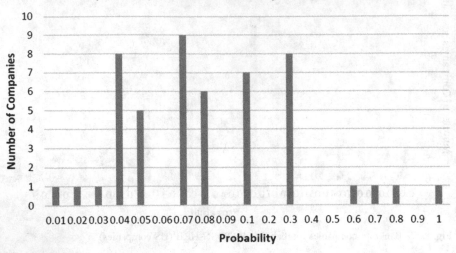

Fig. 8.29 Bankrupt companies' probability, Bayesian model (European companies)

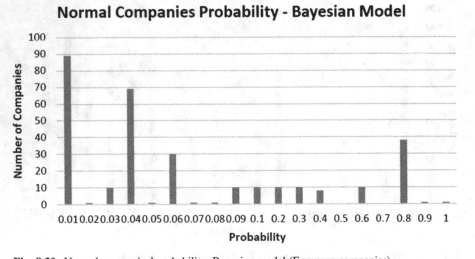

Fig. 8.30 Normal companies' probability, Bayesian model (European companies)

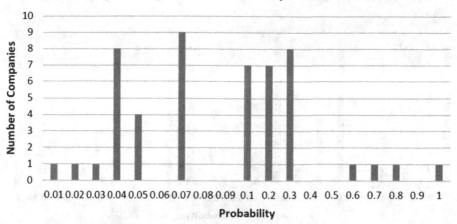

Fig. 8.31 Bankrupt companies' probability, hazard model (European companies)

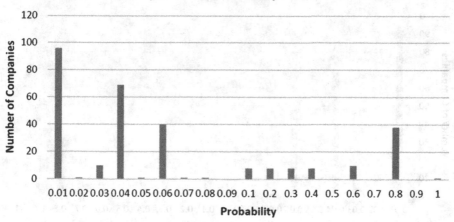

Fig. 8.32 Normal companies' probability, hazard model (European companies)

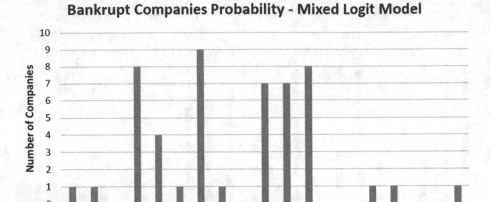

Fig. 8.33 Bankrupt companies' probability, mixed logit model (European companies)

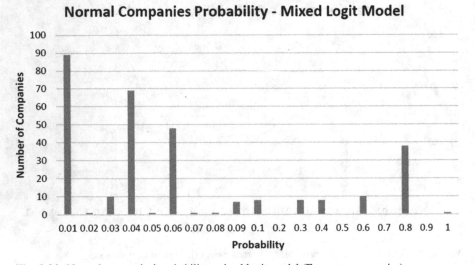

Fig. 8.34 Normal companies' probability, mixed logit model (European companies)

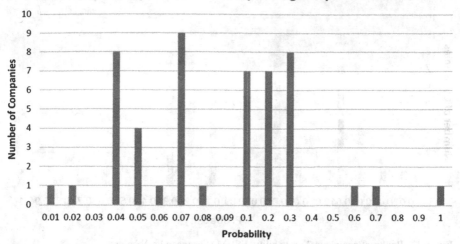

Fig. 8.35   Bankrupt companies' probability, rough Bayesian model (European companies)

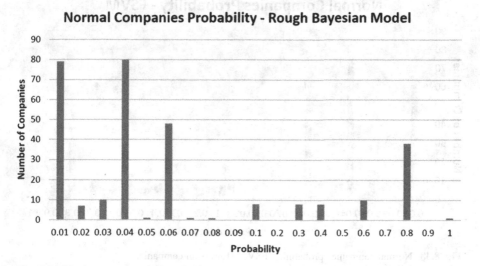

Fig. 8.36   Bankrupt companies' probability, rough Bayesian model (European companies)

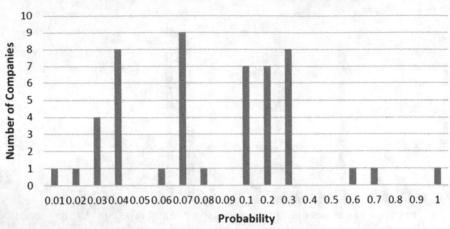

Fig. 8.37 Bankrupt companies' probability, FSVM (European companies)

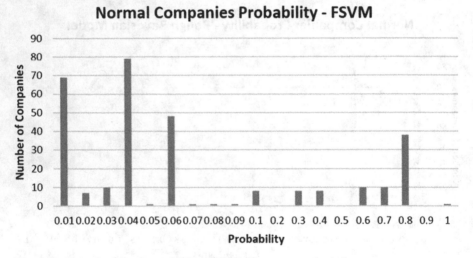

Fig. 8.38 Normal companies probability, FSVM (European companies)

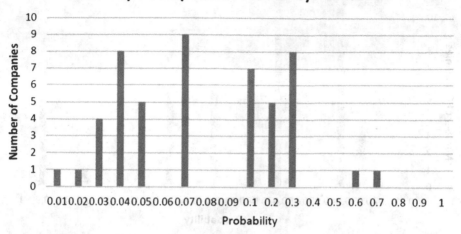

Fig. 8.39   Bankrupt companies probability, MFSVM (European companies)

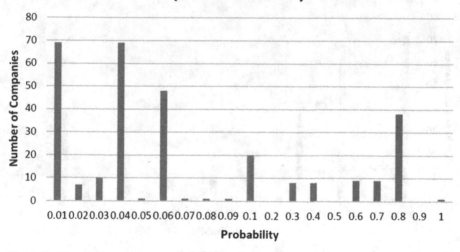

Fig. 8.40   Normal companies probability, MFSVM (European companies)

Bankrupt Companies Probability - FRTDSN-HRB

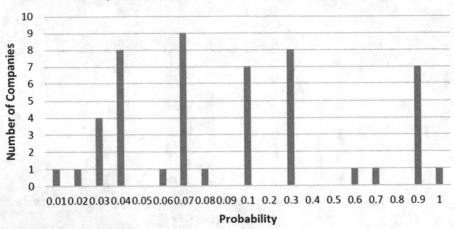

Fig. 8.41 Bankrupt companies probability, FRTDSN-HRB (European companies)

Normal Companies Probability - FRTDSN-HRB

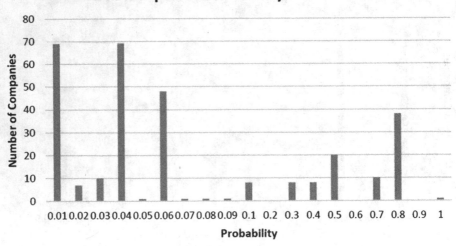

Fig. 8.42 Normal companies probability, FRTDSN-HRB (European companies)

Table 8.19 The results estimated across business cycles (UCI Machine Learning Repository bankruptcy database)

	FRTDSN-HRB		FSVM		MFSVM	
Panel A						
$\frac{Cost_I}{Cost_{II}}$	**1st and 2nd cycle → 3rd cycle**					
	Best	**Normal**	**Best**	**Normal**	**Best**	**Normal**
5	5.4820	0.1429	0.0291	0.0891	0.0750	0.1169
15	0.0119	0.3788	0.0001	0.3685	0.0091	0.2795
25	0.0119	0.4029	0.0001	0.4095	0.0038	0.3650
40	0.0119	0.4300	0.0001	0.4703	0.0030	0.4879
60	0.0119	0.4869	0.0001	0.5319	0.0030	0.5591
80	0.0119	0.5379	0.0001	0.7611	0.0030	0.6209
100	9.6e-3	0.7130	0.0001	0.8630	0.0030	0.7130
Panel B						
$\frac{Cost_I}{Cost_{II}}$	**3rd cycle → 4th cycle**					
	Best	**Normal**	**Best**	**Normal**	**Best**	**Normal**
5	1.5003	0.0709	0.2738	0.0591	0.4019	0.0591
15	0.1879	0.2791	0.0119	0.2030	0.0800	0.3538
25	0.0279	0.5079	0.0079	0.2738	0.0800	0.4987
40	0.0229	0.5569	0.0069	0.3760	0.0619	0.5709
60	0.0229	0.5979	0.0050	0.4679	0.0289	0.5409
80	0.0229	0.6660	0.0050	0.5809	0.0289	0.6091
100	0.0229	0.7338	0.0050	0.6938	0.0289	0.6769

	Bayesian		Hazard		Mixed logit		Rough Bayesian	
Panel A								
$\frac{Cost_I}{Cost_{II}}$	**1st and 2nd cycle → 3rd cycle**							
	Best	**Normal**	**Best**	**Normal**	**Best**	**Normal**	**Best**	**Normal**
5	5.4520	0.1432	0.0292	0.0895	0.0750	0.1171	0.0774	0.1270
15	0.0119	0.3791	0.0002	0.3686	0.0098	0.2795	0.0099	0.2594
25	0.0119	0.4035	0.0002	0.4095	0.0040	0.3552	0.0081	0.3547
40	0.0119	0.4400	0.0002	0.4708	0.0030	0.4582	0.0071	0.4400
60	0.0119	0.4770	0.0002	0.5320	0.0030	0.5192	0.0070	0.5051
80	0.0119	0.5380	0.0001	0.7613	0.0030	0.6211	0.0068	0.6071
100	9.6e-4	0.7230	0.0001	0.8633	0.0030	0.7231	0.0067	0.7351
Panel B								
$\frac{Cost_I}{Cost_{II}}$	**3rd cycle → 4th cycle**							
	Best	**Normal**	**Best**	**Normal**	**Best**	**Normal**	**Best**	**Normal**
5	1.5008	0.0711	0.2740	0.0594	0.4121	0.0596	0.4029	0.0597
15	0.1887	0.2795	0.0129	0.2030	0.0803	0.3538	0.1662	0.2577
25	0.0283	0.5079	0.0086	0.2743	0.0803	0.4987	0.0552	0.4896
40	0.0233	0.5577	0.0074	0.3760	0.0613	0.5719	0.0197	0.3997
60	0.0233	0.5985	0.0058	0.4681	0.0287	0.5419	0.0238	0.5472
80	0.0233	0.6664	0.0058	0.5810	0.0287	0.6092	0.0238	0.6281
100	0.0233	0.7343	0.0058	0.6940	0.0287	0.6772	0.0238	0.7221

Table 8.20 The results estimated across mid-cycles (UCI Machine Learning Repository bankruptcy database)

	FRTDSN-HRB		FSVM		MFSVM	
Panel A						
$\frac{Cost_I}{Cost_{II}}$	**6th mid-cycle → 7th mid-cycle**					
	Best	**Normal**	**Best**	**Normal**	**Best**	**Normal**
5	0.3669	0.1733	0.3672	0.1735	0.3670	0.1734
15	0.1050	0.7585	0.1052	0.7587	0.1050	0.7586
25	0.0730	0.3369	0.0732	0.3371	0.0730	0.3370
40	0.0730	0.5249	0.0732	0.5252	0.0730	0.5250
60	0.0279	0.8279	0.0280	0.8280	0.0279	0.8279
80	0.0279	1.2119	0.0280	1.2120	0.0279	1.2119
100	0.0279	1.5569	0.0280	1.5571	0.0279	1.5570
Panel B						
$\frac{Cost_I}{Cost_{II}}$	**7th mid-cycle → 8th cycle**					
	Best	**Normal**	**Best**	**Normal**	**Best**	**Normal**
5	0.0336	0.1275	0.0336	0.1277	0.0337	0.1276
15	0.0001	0.4036	0.0001	0.4038	0.0001	0.4037
25	0.0001	0.2536	0.0001	0.2538	0.0001	0.2638
40	0.0001	0.3673	0.0001	0.3674	0.0001	0.3674
60	0.0001	0.4895	0.0001	0.4897	0.0001	0.4896
80	0.0001	0.7269	0.0001	0.7270	0.0001	0.7270
100	0.0001	0.8081	0.0001	0.8083	0.0001	0.8081

	Bayesian		Hazard		Mixed logit		Rough Bayesian	
Panel A								
$\frac{Cost_I}{Cost_{II}}$	**6th mid-cycle → 7th mid-cycle**							
	Best	**Normal**	**Best**	**Normal**	**Best**	**Normal**	**Best**	**Normal**
5	0.4034	0.2462	0.2636	0.2675	0.3705	0.1738	0.3674	0.1938
15	0.1964	1.1738	0.0153	0.5351	0.1136	0.8984	0.1054	0.7588
25	0.0830	1.7970	0.0083	0.6900	0.0629	0.3477	0.0734	0.3375
40	0.0196	0.5941	0.0072	1.1266	0.0629	0.5651	0.0734	0.5454
60	0.0196	0.8114	0.0058	1.5491	0.0284	0.8694	0.0286	0.8281
80	0.0196	1.1738	0.0058	2.2534	0.0284	1.2419	0.0286	1.2121
100	0.0196	1.5361	0.0058	2.9576	0.0284	1.6948	0.0286	1.5574
Panel B								
$\frac{C_I}{C_{II}}$	**7th mid-cycle → 8th cycle**							
	Best	**Normal**	**Best**	**Normal**	**Best**	**Normal**	**Best**	**Normal**
5	0.7671	0.1157	0.0002	0.1002	0.0335	0.2404	0.0338	0.1279
15	0.0379	0.6770	0.0001	0.2066	0.0001	0.3920	0.0001	0.4038
25	0.0379	0.6867	0.0001	0.2741	0.0001	0.4801	0.0001	0.2638
40	0.0379	0.7011	0.0001	0.3755	0.0001	0.5 129	0.0001	0.3674
60	0.0379	0.7157	0.0001	0.4870	0.0001	0.6950	0.0001	0.4898
80	0.0379	0.7400	0.0001	0.6464	0.0001	0.7060	0.0001	0.7270
100	0.0379	0.7638	0.0001	0.8669	0.0001	0.8269	0.0001	0.8086

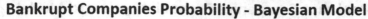

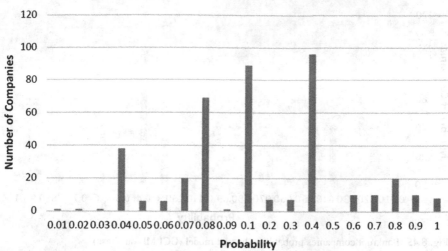

Fig. 8.43   Bankrupt companies probability, Bayesian model (UCI ML database)

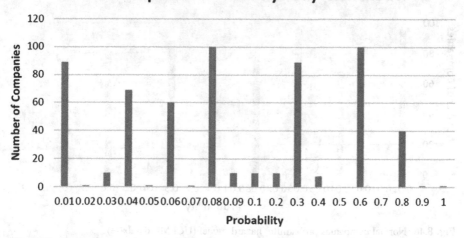

Fig. 8.44   Normal companies probability, Bayesian model (UCI ML database)

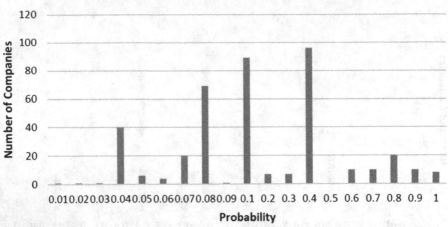

Fig. 8.45 Bankrupt companies probability, hazard model (UCI ML database)

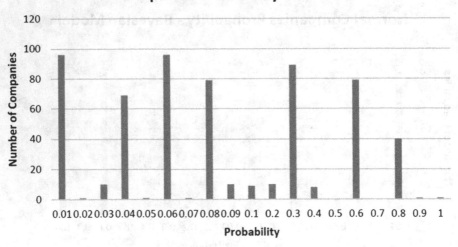

Fig. 8.46 Normal companies probability, hazard model (UCI ML database)

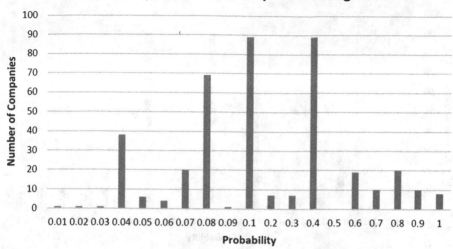

Fig. 8.47 Bankrupt companies probability, mixed logit model (UCI ML database)

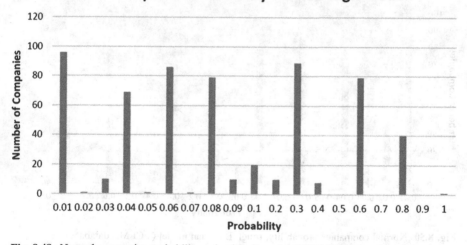

Fig. 8.48 Normal companies probability, mixed logit model (UCI ML database)

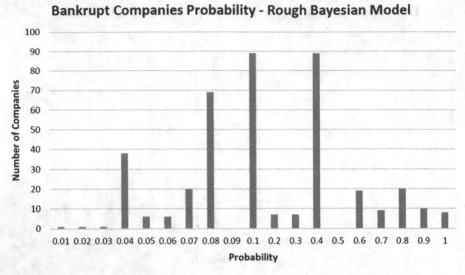

Fig. 8.49 Bankrupt companies probability, rough Bayesian model (UCI ML database)

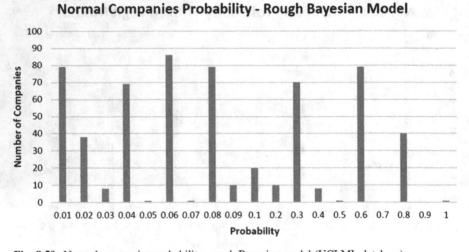

Fig. 8.50 Normal companies probability, rough Bayesian model (UCI ML database)

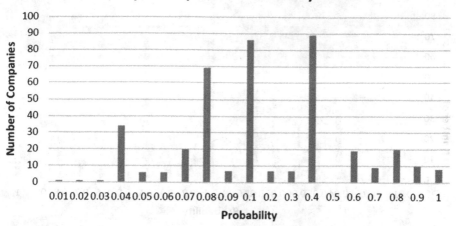

Fig. 8.51   Bankrupt companies probability, FSVM (UCI ML database)

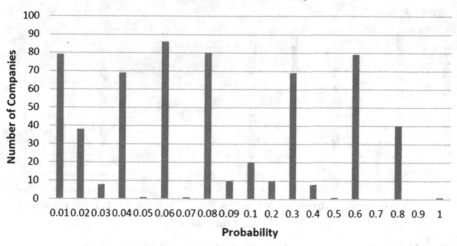

Fig. 8.52   Bankrupt companies probability, FSVM (UCI ML database)

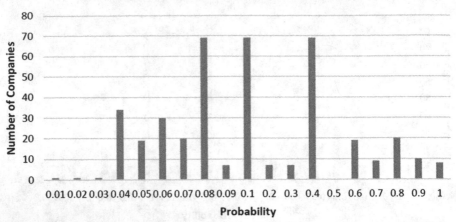

Fig. 8.53 Bankrupt companies probability, MFSVM (UCI ML database)

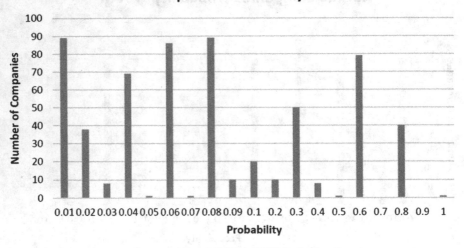

Fig. 8.54 Normal companies probability, MFSVM (UCI ML database)

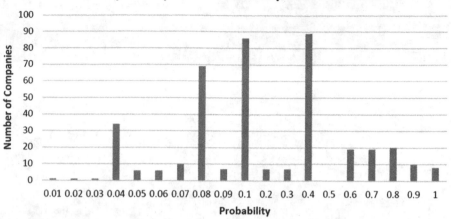

Fig. 8.55 Bankrupt companies probability, FRTDSN-HRB (UCI ML database)

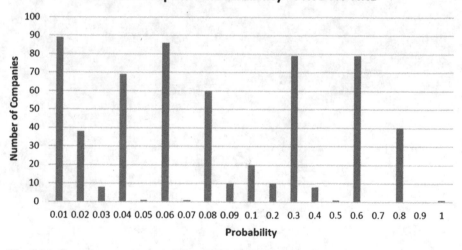

Fig. 8.56 Normal companies probability, FRTDSN-HRB (UCI ML database)

Chapter 9
Conclusion

Here we have proposed complex HDA, viz., FRTDSN-HRB for bankruptcy prediction. FRTDSN is the deep learning model based on TDSN which is made up of multiple stacked blocks where the mapping from input to output through weight tensor higher-order statistics. The learning algorithm of TDSN uses weight matrices and tensors for parameter estimation. The computational power of TDSN is increased by incorporating fuzzy rough sets. HRB are formed by probabilistic rough sets in structured hierarchical Bayesian model where hyperparameter and hyperprior are used in order to achieve the posterior distribution. Then FRTDSN is integrated with HRB which results in FRTDSN-HRB model. HRB enhances the prediction accuracy of FRTDSN-HRB model. All the experiments are performed on the Korean construction companies, American and European nonfinancial companies' datasets, and UCI Machine Learning Repository bankruptcy database. FRTDSN-HRB performance is compared with fuzzy SVMs and other statistical models. To provide a balance in comparison, certain aspects that reduce or grow predictive accuracy are taken care through FRTDSN-HRB model. The cutoff points' selection is affected by backcasting, choice-based sample bias, and change of financial ratio. The prediction results are pushed by the sampling procedure. The arbitrariness level in finding cutoff point is reduced. The optimal cutoff point is used which is calculated by using the training sample as proxy for the real optimal cutoff point. This leads to minimum misclassification cost when compared to cutoff points. The empirical optimal cutoff point denotes that all the models are statistically better in comparison superior to the Bayesian model. This is based on the randomly selected samples when the Type I error cost to Type II error cost ratio is not high. The results are highlighted through several important statistical parameters spread across different business cycles, and mid-cycles illustrate the superiority of the proposed FRTDSN-HRB model. The future research of this work involves development of hybrid soft computing based deep learning models by fine-tuning their parameters such that bankruptcy prediction accuracy is further improved.

A. Chaudhuri, S.K. Ghosh, *Bankruptcy Prediction through Soft Computing based Deep Learning Technique*, https://doi.org/10.1007/978-981-10-6683-2_9

References

1. Altman EL (1993) Corporate financial distress and bankruptcy. Wiley, New York
2. Chaudhuri A (2013) Bankruptcy prediction using Bayesian, hazard, mixed logit and rough Bayesian models: a comparative analysis, computer and information. Science 6(2):103–125
3. Chaudhuri A, De K (2011) Fuzzy support vector machine for bankruptcy prediction. Appl Soft Comput 11(2):2472–2486
4. Altman E (1968) Financial ratios, discriminant analysis and the prediction of corporate bankruptcy. J Financ 23(4):589–609
5. Chaudhuri A (2011) Predicting corporate bankruptcy using soft computing techniques, Technical Report, NIIT University, Neemrana
6. Altman E, Haldeman R, Narayanan P, Analysis ZETA (1977) A new model to identify bankruptcy risk of corporations. J Bank Financ 1(1):29–54
7. Agarwal V, Taffler R (2008) Comparing the performance of market based and accounting based bankruptcy prediction models. J Bank Financ 32(8):1541–1551
8. Altman E (2007) Revisiting credit scoring models in a Basel 2 environment, lecture at National Taiwan University, Available at: www.fin.ntu.edu.tw/~hwangdar/94emba19.ppt
9. Beaver WH, McNichols MF, Rhie JW (2005) Have financial statements become less informative? Evidence from the ability of financial ratios to predict bankruptcy. Rev Acc Stud 10 (1):93–122
10. Bellovary JL, Giacomino D, Akers M (2007) A review of bankruptcy prediction studies: 1930 to present. J Financ Educ 33:1–43
11. Chava S, Jarrow R (2004) Bankruptcy prediction with industry effect, market versus accounting variables and reduced form of credit risk models. Rev Financ 8(4):537–569
12. Hensher DA, Jones S (2007) Forecasting corporate bankruptcy: optimizing the performance of the mixed logit model. Abacus 43(3):241–264
13. Hillegeist S, Cram D, Keating E, Lundstedt K (2004) Assessing the probability of bankruptcy. Rev Acc Stud 9(1):5–34
14. Jones FL (1987) Current techniques in bankruptcy prediction. J Account Lit 6:131–164
15. Martin D (1977) Early warning of Bank failure. J Bank Financ 1(3):249–276
16. McKee TE (2003) Rough sets bankruptcy prediction models versus auditor signaling rates. J Forecast 22(8):569–586
17. Ohlson JA (1980) Financial ratios and probabilistic prediction of bankruptcy. J Account Res 18(1):109–131
18. Ravi Kumar P, Ravi V (2007) Bankruptcy prediction in banks and firms via statistical and intelligent techniques – a review. Eur J Oper Res 180(1):1–28

© Springer Nature Singapore Pte Ltd. 2017
A. Chaudhuri, S.K. Ghosh, *Bankruptcy Prediction through Soft Computing based Deep Learning Technique*, https://doi.org/10.1007/978-981-10-6683-2

19. Sarkar S, Sriram RS (2001) Bayesian models for early warning of Bank failures. Manag Sci 47 (11):1457–1475
20. Shumway T (2001) Forecasting bankruptcy more accurately: a simple hazard model. J Bus 74 (1):101–124
21. Sun L, Shenoy PP (2007) Using Bayesian networks for bankruptcy prediction: some methodological issues. Eur J Oper Res 180(2):738–753
22. Tam KY (1991) Neural network models and the prediction of Bank bankruptcy. Omega 19 (5):429–445
23. Weiss LA, Capkun V (2004) The impact of incorporating the cost of errors into Bankruptcy prediction models. Working Paper
24. Wiginton JC (1980) A note on the comparison of logit and discriminant models of consumer credit behavior. J Financ Quant Anal 15(3):757–770
25. Zavgren C (1983) The prediction of corporate failure: the state of the art. J Account Lit 2 (1):1–37
26. Zmijewski ME (1984) Methodological issues related to the estimation of financial distress prediction models. J Account Res 22(Supplement):59–82
27. Jones S, Hensher DA (2004) Predicting firm financial distress: a mixed logit model. Account Rev 79(4):1011–1038
28. Goodfellow I, Bengio Y, Courville A (2016) Deep learning. MIT Press, Cambridge
29. Patterson J, Gibson A (2016) Deep learning: a Practitioner's approach, 1st edn. O'Reilly, Sebastopol
30. Burges CJC (1998) A tutorial on support vector machine for pattern recognition, vol 1–43. Kluwer Academic Publishers, Boston
31. Hutchinson B, Deng L, Yu D (2013) Tensor deep stacking networks. IEEE Trans Pattern Anal Mach Intell 35(8):1944–1957
32. Korean Construction Companies Dataset: NICE DnB http://www.nicednb.com
33. Hajek P, Michalak K (2013) Feature selection in corporate credit rating prediction. Knowl Based Syst 51:72–84
34. Myoung JK, Ingoo H (2003) The discovery of experts' decision rules from qualitative bankruptcy data using genetic algorithms. Expert Syst Appl 25(4):637–646
35. Chaudhuri A (2014) Modified fuzzy support vector machine for credit approval classification. AI Commun 27(2):189–211
36. Smith R, Winakor A (1935) Changes in financial structure of unsuccessful industrial corporations, Bureau of Business Research, bulletin number 51. University of Illinois Press, Urbana
37. Merwin C (1942) Financing small corporations in five manufacturing industries, 1926–1936. National Bureau of Economic Research, New York
38. Hickman WB (1965) Corporate bond quality and investor experience. Princeton University Press, Princeton
39. Beaver WH (1966) Financial ratios as predictors of failure. Empir Res Account Sel Stud:71–111
40. Weiss L A, Capkun V (2004) The impact of incorporating the cost of errors into Bankruptcy Prediction models. Working Paper
41. Deakin E (1972) A discriminant analysis of predictors of business failure. J Account Res 10 (1):167–179
42. Wilcox A (1971) A simple theory of financial ratios as predictors of failure. J Account Res 9 (3):389–395
43. Begley J, Ming J, Watts S (1996) Bankruptcy classification errors in the 1980s: an empirical analysis of Altman's and Ohlson's models. Rev Acc Stud 1(4):267–284
44. Mensah YM (1984) An examination of the stationarity of multivariate bankruptcy prediction models: a methodological study. J Account Res 22(1):380–395
45. Webster E, Thornton DB (2005) Earnings quality under rules versus principles based accounting standards: a test of the skinner hypothesis. Can Account Perspect 4(2):167–192

46. Ramser J, Foster L (1931) A demonstration of ratio analysis, Bulletin 40, University of Illinois, Bureau of Business Research, Urbana
47. Fitzpatrick P (1932) A comparison of the ratios of successful industrial enterprises with those of failed organizations. The Accounting Publishing Company, Washington
48. Winakor A, Smith R (1935) Changes in the financial structure of unsuccessful industrial corporations, Bulletin 51, University of Illinois, Bureau of Business Research, Urbana
49. Merton R (1974) On the pricing of corporate debt: the risk structure of interest rates. J Financ 29(2):449–470
50. Koh HC, Tan SS (1999) A neural network approach to the prediction of going concern status. Account Bus Res 29(3):211–216
51. Atiya AF (2001) Bankruptcy prediction for credit risk using neural networks: a survey and new results. IEEE Trans Neural Netw 12(4):929–935
52. Baek J, Cho S (2003) Bankruptcy prediction for credit risk using an auto-associative neural network in Korean firms. In: Proceedings of the CIFEr, Hong Kong, pp 25–29
53. Becerra VM, Galvao RKH, Abou-Seads M (2005) Neural and wavelet network models for financial distress classification. Data Min Knowl Disc 11(1):35–55
54. Durga L, Dimitri P (2006) Machine learning approaches for estimation of prediction interval for the model output. Neural Netw 19(2):225–235
55. Pramodh C, Ravi V (2007) Modified great deluge algorithm based auto-associative neural network for bankruptcy prediction in banks. Int J Comput Intell Res 3(4):363–370
56. Purvinis O, Šukys P, Virbickaitė P (2005) Research of possibility of bankruptcy diagnostics applying neural network. Eng Econ 41(1):16–22
57. Ravi V, Kumar PR, Srinivas ER, Kasabov NK (2007) A semi-online training algorithm for the radial basis function neural networks: applications to bankruptcy prediction in banks. In: Ravi V (ed) Advances in banking technology and management: impact of ICT and CRM. IGI Global, Hershey
58. Shah JR, Mirza BM (2000) A neural network based clustering procedure for bankruptcy prediction. Am Bus Rev 18(2):80–86
59. Quinlan JR (1986) Induction of decision trees. Mach Learn 1(1):81–106
60. Frydman H, Altman E, Kao DL (1985) Introducing recursive partitioning for financial classification: the case of financial distress. J Financ 40(1):269–291
61. Artificial Neural Networks: https://en.wikipedia.org/wiki/Artificial_neural_network
62. Backpropagation: https://en.wikipedia.org/wiki/Backpropagation
63. Odom M, Sharda R (1990) A neural network for bankruptcy prediction. In: Proceedings of the IJCNN International Conference on Neural Networks, San Diego, pp 163–168
64. Tam K, Kiang M (1992) Managerial application of neural networks: the case of bank failure prediction. Manag Sci 38(7):926–947
65. Darwin's Theory of Evolution: https://en.wikipedia.org/wiki/Darwinism
66. Lensberg T, Eilifsen A, McKee TE (2006) Bankruptcy theory development and classification via genetic programming. Eur J Oper Res 169(2):677–697
67. Sengupta RN, Singh R (2007) Bankruptcy prediction using artificial immune systems. In: DeCastro LN, Zuben FJ, Knidel H (eds) Artificial immune systems, lecture notes in computer science, vol 4628. Springer, Berlin, pp 131–141
68. Kumar PR, Ravi V (2006) Bankruptcy prediction in banks by fuzzy rule based classifier. In: Proceedings of 1st IEEE International Conference on Digital and Information Management, Bangalore, pp 222–227
69. Shin KS, Lee TS, Kim HJ (2005) An application of support vector machines in bankruptcy prediction model. Expert Syst Appl 28(1):127–135
70. Dimitras A, Slowinski R, Susmaga R, Zopounidis C (1999) Business failure prediction using rough sets. Eur J Oper Res 114(2):263–280
71. Bioch JC, Popova V (2001) Bankruptcy prediction with rough sets, EIRM Report Series Research in Management

72. Ruzgar NS, Unsal F, Ruzgar B (2008) Predicting bankruptcies using rough set approach: the case of Turkish banks. In: Proceedings of American Conference on Applied Mathematics, Harvard
73. Shuai JJ, Li HL (2005) Using rough set and worst practice DEA in business failure prediction. In: Ślezak D et al (eds) Rough sets, fuzzy sets, data mining and granular computing, lecture notes in computer science, vol 3642. Springer, Berlin/New York, pp 503–510
74. Zaini BJ, Shamsuddin SM, Jaaman SH (2008) Comparison between rough set theory and logistic regression for classifying firm's performance. J Qual Meas Anal 4(1):141–153
75. Ahn H, Kim KJ (2009) Bankruptcy prediction modeling with hybrid case based reasoning and genetic algorithms approach. Appl Soft Comput 9(2):599–607
76. Jo H, Han I, Lee H (1997) Bankruptcy prediction using case based reasoning, neural networks, and discriminant analysis. Expert Syst Appl 13(2):97–108
77. Ravi V, Kurniawan H, NweeKok TP, Kumar PR (2008) Soft computing system for bank performance prediction. Appl Soft Comput J 8(1):305–315
78. Ryu YU, Yue WT (2005) Firm bankruptcy prediction: experimental comparison of isotonic separation and other classification approaches, IEEE transactions on systems, man and cybernetics. Syst Humans 35(5):727–737
79. Tung WL, Queka C, Cheng P, GenSo EWS (2004) A novel neural fuzzy based early warning system for predicting bank failures. Neural Netw 17:567–587
80. Vlachos D, Tollias YA (2003) Neuro fuzzy modeling in bankruptcy prediction. Yugoslav J Oper Res 13(2):165–174
81. Wu CH, Tseng GH, Goo YJ, Fang WC (2007) A real valued genetic algorithm to optimize the parameters of support vector machine for predicting bankruptcy. Expert Syst Appl 32 (2):397–408
82. Deep Learning: https://en.wikipedia.org/wiki/Deep_learning
83. Bankruptcy Prediction: https://en.wikipedia.org/wiki/Bankruptcy_prediction
84. Vapnik VN (1995) The nature of statistical learning theory. Springer, New York
85. Hierarchical Bayesian Model: https://en.wikipedia.org/wiki/Bayesian_hierarchical_modeling
86. Pawlak Z (1991) Rough sets, theoretical aspects of reasoning about data. Kluwer Academic Publishers, Dordrecht
87. Chaudhuri A (2016) Fuzzy rough support vector machine for data classification. Int J Fuzzy Syst Appl 5(2):26–53
88. Yao YY (2010) Three way decisions with probabilistic rough sets. Inf Sci 180(3):341–353
89. Yao YY (2008) Probabilistic rough set approximations. Int J Approx Reason 49(2):255–271
90. Yao YY (2007) Decision Theoretic Rough Set models. In: Proceedings of RSKT 2007, Lecture Notes in Artificial Intelligence, LNAI 4481, pp 1–12
91. Yao YY, Wong SKM, Decision Theoretic A (1992) Framework for approximating concepts. Int J Man Mach Stud 37(6):793–809
92. Yao YY, Wong SKM, Lingras PA (1990) Decision theoretic rough set model. In: Ras ZW, Zemankova M, Emrich ML (eds) Methodologies for intelligent systems 5. North Holland, New York, pp 17–24

Printed in the United States
By Bookmasters